The Big Blue Turtle

The Meaning of Life and How to Survive Death

MATTHEW COLERIDGE

Fulton Books, Inc.
Meadville, PA

Published by Fulton Books 2021

ISBN 978-1-63710-818-5 (paperback)
ISBN 978-1-63710-819-2 (digital)

Printed in the United States of America

For my mother,
this is what I wanted to tell you as you prepared to cross the Veil.

INTRODUCTION

This book does not have to be read in a linear fashion. That is, you can skip around and read from any point, wherever it may catch your eye. The universe is not linear, and there is no plot to this story. Nothing unfolds—it is all laid out for you to discover as you explore. And I am a bit scatterbrained these days for reasons that I will get into at points in this book, so my thought process isn't linear, either. I started to write this as a story with characters and a plot, a story about a woman who hits rock bottom but then discovers the real purpose of this existence and realizes her importance within it. It started off well enough, but all the details that needed to be worked in did not fit a linear plot very well. My reasons for abandoning the story format boils down to Lewis Carroll and Kurt Vonnegut.

The thing that has always kept me from writing this down has been the question "Where do I begin?" Lewis Carroll famously wrote, "Begin at the beginning," but I can't ever decide where the beginning should be. I have been, for many attempts over the years, what Kurt Vonnegut referred to as a "basher"—someone who bashes out a bit of a story, stops, has doubts, and deletes everything to begin again. He suggested being a "swooper"—someone who just swoops in, writes what needs to be said, and then cleans it up later, thereby actually getting the thing done. I will attempt that with this try. So what makes this try different?

The difference is that I do not know how much time I have left in this life. And this may be my last chance to put this down in print for others to read, consider, and then adopt the entirety, adopt the bits they like or discard it entirely. My responsibility lies only with giving you that option. Am I dying? Well, I have certainly been thinking about it a lot lately. Each night as I lie in bed, I tell myself,

"I'm dying." And it's not a sad thing for me to consider. It comes more along the lines of "Well, my life didn't go the way I had wanted it to. That sucks. But I don't care. I'm dying." Death is just another experience. Still, it is odd to think of the world without me. I'll miss all my favorite shows, all the books I never got to read, and all the new movies I'll never see—places I will never visit. That one's not such a sticker because I have visited far more places than most people get to see. And the people—I will miss them most of all. I will also miss the animals. Actually, I won't really miss any of them as they continue on as everything does, in some form or another. I suppose what I will really miss is my life, and what is life but the experiences we have and the memories we make? So this book explains how you can take them with you. They are the only things you can take with you, after all. They *are* you.

I've reached the full midlife point: fifty years of age. Some of the more generous among you may say that fifty is not that old. But consider this: I have already outlived my father by four years, and he handed some genetic curses down to me, which include but are not limited to hypertension and heart disease. I have been taking medication for my blood pressure since college. I have been living in Korea now for about thirteen years, off and on (broken up by brief periods spent in Oman and in my home country, the likely-doomed USA). Korea has a particularly good health-care system, as does Oman, unlike the likely-doomed USA (oh, America's system is fine if you're wealthy, but this would set me off on a political tangent, so I will just leave this here in parenthesis), and my doctors here tell me that I have likely suffered at least one heart attack in the past few years based on scarring on the lower left chamber of my heart. Apparently, you can have a heart attack and not realize it. I was in Seoul two years ago to celebrate Halloween with some friends, and I had a nagging ache in my sternum for much of the night. I had sweats that came and went, and I felt slightly nauseous, so I went home early and rested. The next morning, I felt fine, but I figured as long as I was in Seoul near my doctor, I would pop in just for a quick checkup. They ran an EKG and did some blood work and told me my results would be ready in two hours. I went into the shopping district near

Severance Hospital and had lunch then went back up to the hospital to get my test results. As soon as I walked in, they rushed me to the cardio-intensive care unit, and I spent three days under observation, receiving two CT scans and a cardiac catheterization before being released. In America, this would have cost me over seventy thousand dollars. In South Korea, it cost me seven hundred dollars. But again, I don't want to make this political.

Seven years before this, I had a similar occurrence in my apartment one night when I felt a sharp, prolonged stabbing pain in my sternum. I rode it out as it was past midnight, despite the fact that there was a hospital right beside my apartment building. That pain had subsided after an hour or so, and I had forgotten about it, chalking it up to some sort of gastrointestinal issue. It may very well have been much more than that. Today, whenever I feel even a slight twinge in my chest or upper torso, I think, "Oh shit, here we go!" and who knows—one of these times, we may just.

The point is, none of us really knows when our number is going to come up, and these days, I am acutely aware of my mortality, so I figured it was time to stop bashing and start swooping and get this message in a bottle out to whomever may need it.

What I am going to tell you in this small book is something that I am not supposed to tell anyone. I just realized that I wrote earlier: *The thing that has always kept me from writing this down has been the question "Where do I begin?"* That is largely true, but it is not the whole truth. There has also always been something there that prevented me from writing it, something more than mere indecision. In fact, on the night that I finally decided to share it, I had a terrible nightmare. I was lying in bed thinking about mortality, as one does before sleep, and I said to myself, "I need to write this down while I have the chance." And I fell asleep. And the nightmare came. It was the weirdest nightmare I have ever had, and I am not really prone to nightmares. I have vivid dreams sometimes, but nothing terrifying as this was. The dream consisted of me feeling like I was tripping on LSD. Having done this many times in my twenties, this is not the scary part. I quite enjoyed my trips on LSD and psilocybin mushrooms and cannabis.

7

While I prefer organic hallucinogens, LSD has never been anything but nice to me. However, in this nightmare, as I watched the world around me distorted by swirling eddies of hallucination, I distinctly recall knowing that this was never going to end, that this was me losing my sanity, or dying. I was aware I was dreaming, but the overall feeling was that this would become my reality upon my death. Horrific, demonic faces appeared in the swirling eddies, screamed at me, and were gone. I recorded it fresh when I woke up, and as I write this, I am listening to my recorded account from my own sleepy voice. I was running from evil entities through a city scene of odd-angled buildings with cars and rubble scattered in the street. Under some trees, there was a gazebo that was full of people. I mention arguing about free will with someone dressed in a flashy green robe and carrying a staff. I ran looking for my mother (who died from Parkinson's disease in 2012) to tell her that I was going insane.

This was it for me, one too many trips down the rabbit hole and this time I would not be coming back out. The feeling of strong hallucinations continued all around me, and I ran to the gazebo because there were some people there, and one of them said to me, "You need to read Arthur C. Clark," and I woke up. The only real takeaway was the feeling of terror I felt during the dream as well as upon waking. It scared me so much I grabbed my phone and recorded it, but it's a first-waking account of a dream. If you have ever read any books about dreams and dream interpretation, then you may have read that being aware that you are having a nightmare within a dream is a sign of deep psychosis. So that should be encouraging. "Listen to me. I'm crazy!" I was aware I was dreaming of a nightmare, and I was also aware that this was being foisted on me by what some might call demons, and it was punishment for deciding to share what I know about life and death. I was breaching some sort of nondisclosure agreement, and the punishment was this version of hell, the loss of the mind, which is the soul: it is YOU. The last thing I say in the recording is an evocation to Christ and a request for protection from all the archangels. I'm a little dramatic when I first wake up. I decided to write this all down anyway and began writing these notes. A few days later, I woke up from a dreamless sleep (I am certain

I dreamed—we always do, I figure—I just didn't recall any of the dreams) and found my desk covered in a puddle of water. My laptop was dead. And the damnedest thing was, there was nothing around the desk or laptop—no spilled water bottle, nothing. I couldn't figure out where the water had come from. Was it like one of those locked door mysteries, where some ice had melted on my desk? Had a pipe in the ceiling broken during the night? There were no water stains up there. Had I woken up during the night and pissed on my laptop? It didn't smell like piss. It didn't smell like anything, just water. And I really like water—I have always had a deep affinity for water. There is something miraculous about water, as if it has a consciousness all its own. I will talk about that later. I do not, however, like water interacting with my electronics.

All this—the nightmare, the drowned laptop—happened over a month ago, about three weeks before Christmas. Today is January 5, 2021. I chalked it up to the popular 2020 curse. But now I am writing again and hoping hell doesn't come for my new laptop.

There's a concept: hell. I will talk about this as we go forward, but for right now, let me just tell you that the Christian vision of hell is nonexistent. The newer vision of hell inspired by Dante is also nonexistent. There really is no literal version of hell unless you create it for yourself. A lot of the hot biblical takes that are bandied about in modern religion are gross misrepresentations of a larger truth. I will discuss these as we go.

Keep in mind as you read this work that I will go off on tangents as there is a lot to cover, and this is how my thought process conducts itself these days. I will jump around, but I will always come back to the central theme—the topics of the title of this book—eventually. Just be patient with me as this is a rush job, and we do have a lot to consider. And feel free to jump around yourself.

Also, I will refer to many facts and accounts as I go, and I will speak of them as if I assume you are already aware of them. Some of you may very well be. For the rest, I did not go into a lot of detail on some of these accounts because we are living in the miraculous Age of Information, and you are encouraged to do your own research. If you are interested in learning more about anything that I may mention in passing, google it. It is all available online, along with a lot more that I will not share here for the sake of staying on topic. Most of these side references are worthy of books on their own merit, and many of them are already the subjects of books—thousands of them—so go get 'em. The point of this book is not to convince you of the larger reality of our world—there is ample supporting evidence out there if you care to look. Some people feel safer not knowing about it, others feel a great sense of relief when they do. The point of this book is simply to add my voice to the call of concern that all of us should be hearing by now. We face a global pandemic that, despite vaccinations, does not appear to be going away any time soon and which may get worse. People are dying in the hundreds of thousands. I would only hope that this book might give them some comfort. Even when this pandemic subsides, there will likely be another. Democracy has faced a very bad year as people are not just forced to give up their voice in how they are governed but seem to do so willingly. And the problems we are causing our environment are not going away, nor are the myriad of other problems we face as a species. War, famine, poverty—water has just become a commodity! Think about that. Our world is headed down a dark path, and there is nothing I can do about it except write this here for you to read.

Having said all that, let me now say that everything I will write here is the truth as I understand it. However, I could be wrong. I really, truly do not think that I am because I was told everything that I am going to tell you by a higher consciousness, and it was shared with me over the course of several lifetimes.

How did that last line grab you? Crazy, right? Well, hang on, because I am going to tell you everything that I am not supposed to tell, and it may sound absolutely insane to most of you. A lot of this will not be new information for a lot of you. But hear me out. You may be glad that you did. Either way, I hope you enjoy the ride.

CHAPTER 1

The Biggest Truths

This will be a very short chapter because, as I said in the introduction, I want to stay on topic, and this bit is simple enough and should be remembered. Let's begin with the biggest truths of this book right off the bat because who knows how long any of us have. This will not be like one of those scam internet videos that keeps saying, "Keep watching this video, and I will tell you how to realize your greatest dreams!" That's bullshit. I will get straight to the point. So let's get right to it, shall we?

The biggest truths:

1. There are only *Two Rules of Life*:
    i.   Never harm any other sentient being, physically or emotionally. If you do (and you likely will at this stage of the game), apologize.
    ii. Never, ever enforce your opinions, beliefs, or ideologies on others. Live how you choose but allow others the same courtesy.
2. *The Meaning of Life*: This world, this experience of life, is a school. You are here to learn to be better, more capable, and more powerful souls. You are here to learn how to perfect your consciousness so that you may join with other perfected consciousnesses to form a collective consciousness, a "universal mind," and this will be God. I use the term "God" for lack of a better term, something akin to a conscious universe or universal consciousness. As we will

get into later, the God or gods mentioned in our collective histories are likely just entities far more advanced than ourselves. As for our collective consciousness, we are talking about reproduction on a cosmic scale: the procreation of universal consciousness, gods (read: conscious universes) creating gods, if you will—or, perhaps, a god beyond time creating itself. As the esoteric paraphrase of the second verse of the *Emerald Tablet* suggests, "as above, so below." You are here in a physical form to learn to develop *integrity*, not only regarding your character but in your ability to hold your consciousness—your soul—together once outside the physical mold (body). We will be talking a lot about how to develop this integrity so that you may survive outside the physical. This is how you survive death and attain that eternal life that all religions seem to promise but never really deliver. I am going to tell you how to do that. And this is why I may be in trouble.

3.   The Bible is a broken text. It still contains a few remnants of the truths it once was meant to convey, but it has been mistranslated, retranslated, and edited by kings and tyrants since its inception. Entire books have been removed. We will look at what is left, which isn't much, but it is still sacred.

4.   You should not fear death. It's nothing you haven't experienced before. Those memories are just walled off from your conscious self for this trip around so that you can develop aspects of your soul that are wanting.

5.   This one I got from a bumper sticker I saw at a Grateful Dead concert, but it is truth: *You do not have a soul. You ARE a soul. You HAVE a body.*

There we are, we'll leave it at the first five that occurred to me. There will be other truths revealed as we continue, but I feel those are the big ones. Continue reading to see if you agree with my assessment.

So where to begin? Let's begin with the beginning of the Bible, specifically, the first words spoken by God in Genesis 1:3: *L et there be light.*

CHAPTER 2

Let There Be Light

Before it was fractured by corrupted hands, the Bible was intended to be a collection of multilayered texts. For the beginner, the uniniti-ated, it was meant to be a collection of historical details, simple rules, and parables to help guide one onto the path of a perfected soul. To the initiated, it contained symbolic truths hidden within the simple text, and this symbolism also held advanced scientific knowledge, often indicated by the repetition of prime numbers like 3, 5, and 7. Prime numbers indicate a truth. The number 40 is also a sacred number, and it represents a period of probation and trial. The num-ber 40 is mentioned 146 times in scripture. It rained on Noah's ark for 40 days and 40 nights, the Jews wandered in the desert for 40 years, and Jesus fasted in the desert for 40 days. There are several aca-demic papers available that explain the significance of certain num-bers in the pages of the Bible, as well as the Apocryphon, those books the church removed from the Bible because they contained passages that did not agree with their view or posed a threat to their control.

Parable and analogy also play a big role in the text. The tale of Jesus turning water into wine is analogous to the process of photo-synthesis: the sun (here as symbolic Son of God) turns water into wine via the grapes taking nourishment from the leaves producing energy through photosynthesis. In this way, the Bible was meant to be seen more as a symbolic text, not as a literal historical account. Among its more basic literal interpretations, the Bible offered a way for ascended masters, scholars, and higher consciousnesses to conceal what may have been considered sensitive information. Artists such as da Vinci did the same with their works. Any information truly worth having is always hidden.

The concept of the Son of God representing the actual sun is common in studies of the Bible: it gives sight to the blind, it raises the dead (in terms of much of the natural world dying in the winter only to be rejuvenated in the spring), and if you've ever marveled at sunshine on the water as John Denver did, then you could say the sun walked on the water. And it can reveal things once hidden, just as Jesus did, and let's put that down right away, his name was *not* "Jesus." There is no J in the Aramaic alphabet. His name was Yeshua. Jesus is an Italian mistranslation of the Greek J, which was pronounced as Y. So all these "Christians" praying to Jesus, they've got the wrong guy there.

I am not trying to suggest that Yeshua did not perform the miracles attributed to him. His awesome deeds could very well be what inspired his comparison to the sun, which had represented God itself not long before. And I have no idea what occult knowledge Yeshua had learned in his studies. I am using the true definition of the word *occult* here: it simply means "hidden." The movie industry and pop culture have really screwed with our understanding of the true etymology of much of our language. I know Yeshua was a powerful priest, a member of an order of high initiates, he may have even been a higher entity himself. But I also know that many of the accounts of Yeshua's life are borrowed from earlier god-king deities who were also called sons of God. Krishna, for example, has a life story that matches that of Yeshua to a T, and yet he lived a thousand years prior. Other sons of God with similar backstories include Tammuz, Adonis, and Osiris. Perhaps these stories were simply attributed to Yeshua to further legitimize his claim as the Messiah? Either way, it does not, in my opinion, detract from the power and significance of Yeshua or his message.

On the subject of the sun and vineyards, I would be remiss if I did not mention the famous parable of the bad tenants. This parable appears in the gospels of Matthew, Mark, Luke, and (noncanonical) Thomas, so I can only assume it is important. This is the story told by Yeshua of the landlord who builds a beautiful vineyard and rents it out to some farmers. When harvest time comes, the landlord sends his slave(s) to collect his share of the fruit. The tenants beat, stone, and kill one or more slaves (depending on the version), so the landlord sends more slaves. These people (or person) meet the same nasty reception. Finally, the landlord sends his son, figuring the tenants will have to respect his heir. But no. The tenants figure, "Hey, this guy is the boss's son! Let's kill him and take his inheritance!" Disregarding the idiocy of this plan (What did they think the landlord was going to say? "Oh, you killed my son! Looks like you're entitled to his inheritance!"), the important thing is that they do, indeed, murder the landlord's son. Now most biblical scholars consider this parable in regard to supporting Yeshua's death in his role as Messiah. The true message should be regarded in terms of the earth itself and how we—the tenants—take care of the environment.

The duty of humanity as the caretakers of this planet is paramount. And we have been sorely lacking in this duty. We are killing the environment that has been so painstakingly bestowed upon this earth. Most contactee messages carry a dire warning about environmental issues and stress the importance of keeping the place clean (as any landlord would advise their tenants). As the members of Yeshua's audience note, one would expect the landlord to expel the bad tenants and find more responsible renters. If you think Yeshua is making idle threats, I refer you to the many previous civilizations that are now submerged beneath our planet's oceans. What happened to those people? Bad tenants? This is also the parable in which Yeshua speaks of the stone that the builders refused. It seems a bit off-topic at the end of this parable about farmers. To me, it reeks of the sort of shoddy editing done by those covering something up. It seems more fitting to a parable about builders rather than farmers, but who am I to judge? Look at my own shoddy storytelling abilities. But the mention of this stone also may be another case of multilayered symbolism, the "as above, so below" maxim. The Hebrew word for "son" is *ben*, which is very similar to the word for "stone," *eben*. This could refer to the radical concept that people (i.e., sons and daughters) are not to be tossed aside as disposable. We are no more disposable than the planet we have been entrusted with. The points on our heads that align with the pineal gland (the "third eye," or our spiritual eye) are called "temples." Our bodies, like our earth, are meant to be seen as sacred and must remain unpolluted. We have been doing a pretty lousy job of protecting both. What we do to the earth, we do to ourselves. I guess my point here is that we all must help in some way to protect the environment. This is of tremendous importance. When a messenger comes with a warning about how we are neglecting our responsibilities as tenants, no matter how insignificant the corporate elite may seem to consider them (say, a group of Native Americans or a young girl from Sweden), *heed their words.* Don't reject these stones as they will become the foundation of something better.

What was I talking about? Ah, yes, light.

When God says "Let there be light" at the beginning of the Bible, they had already created the heavens and the earth, so there was already, presumably, the sun. As this is the first line spoken by God, it means to the initiated that there is a second meaning here. In artwork throughout human history, light represents knowledge. This is why enlightened beings such as Jesus, Buddha, Muhammad, and angels are pictured with halos of light emanating from their heads. This is also why a light bulb appears above Ziggy's head when he has an idea—light is symbolic of knowledge. This is why we say things like "What a brilliant idea!" and "She's a very bright student." And on the opposite end of the stick, "to be kept in the dark" means to be kept ignorant of some fact, or to say someone is a "dim bulb" means they are "not too bright" or unintelligent. The Dark Ages were a time of deep ignorance—held in place by the church itself, which shredded the Bible at the Council of Nicaea in AD 325, and largely destroyed the actual, factual teachings of Yeshua to keep the masses in darkness so that the church could maintain its hold on Europe.

What God is saying in Genesis 1:3 is, "Let there be knowledge," as in "this book contains information you will need." At least, it used to before popes, emperors, and kings got their corrupt little fingers on it.

Aside from light, another symbol of knowledge is the apple. This is why we see apples depicted in cartoons and clip art related to school. There's always an apple on the teacher's desk. This is where the parable of Sir Isaac Newton getting beaned on the noggin by a falling apple came from—it represents an epiphany, but it never actually happened. This brings us to the most infamous apple in the story: the piece of fruit taken from the tree of knowledge and eaten by Eve in the garden of Eden in Genesis. This, too, is heavily symbolic, and I hope you see why. This brings us to another great truth.

The serpent in the garden of Eden was the *good* guy. The "God" of the Old Testament wanted to keep early humans (represented by Adam and Eve) ignorant, naked, and afraid. The serpent, on the other hand, tried to educate the humans, teaching them how they could evolve and become like "gods" themselves. The serpent represented a particular house or organization of "gods" credited in the myths of many cultures with the creation of our species. This is why the Caduceus, or Staff of Hermes, still survives as the symbol of the American Medical Association. It depicts two serpents intertwined to form the double helix of DNA (although a recent rebrand has reduced it to just one serpent because they feared the original symbol was a bit on the nose). All the old "gods" are often blended into one centralized figure for the ease and simplification of storytelling. Incidentally, the serpent was not Satan, and Satan is not Lucifer. Although the name Lucifer does mean "light-bringer," Lucifer is a different entity, but lazy translation and summarization from the early church blended them into the same character for their story. The church and other organized religions flipped the script because they liked the way that the Old Testament God ran things, and they wanted to maintain that sort of control over their flocks—keep them obedient, tithe-paying, and killing on command. Consider the traditional pose of prayer: on your knees, head down, hands together as if in bondage. This is how early humans were brought before this "God." The serpent secretly tried to teach the humans how they could rise from the bondage of servitude and to know the same things that this "God" knows. (I do not use the past tense "knew" here because this entity still exists.)

Lucifer is also known as Morning Star, which is a reference to Venus. These outside entities were often associated with astrological markers and phenomena so as to make it easier for early humans to learn about the world beyond Earth. As Venus orbits the sun, it traces out a lobed pentagram every thirteen years (as opposed to eight orbits completed by the Earth). This is known as the pentagram of Venus, and this is how the pentagram became known as the symbol of Lucifer, and erroneously Satan, and why the number thirteen carries such superstitious potency. The lobed pentagram looks very different from the pentagram used in campy "Black Magic" rituals. The actual pentagram of Venus, with its lobes, looks more like a flower. The "magic" pentagram is the pointy one that is often traced around a goat head.

Speaking of goats, always remember that words have power—real power. So choose them wisely. Always think before you speak, especially in this day and age when everything is recorded online for posterity. Go ahead and delete that offensive tweet—it'll still come back to bite you on the ass. Words often change over time, and their power changes too. Look at the word "nice," as in "What a nice guy!" In Shakespeare's time, to say someone was "nice" was to say they were silly or ridiculous. "Nice guys finish last!" Story of my life. Anyway, I find it curious that the word "goat," especially how it is used in sports references, has changed. When I was growing up, to say you were the "goat" meant that you were the loser, you were the one who scored a goal for the other team or otherwise lost the game. Today, it has changed to an acronym meaning "greatest of all time." I wonder if that is purposeful? This has been a tangent. Thank you for riding along.

Another problematic translation in the Bible is the word "God" itself. Have you ever wondered why, if there is only one God, Genesis 1:26 says, "Let *us* make man in *our* image?" This is no mistake. The church tries to explain this away by saying it refers to the Holy Trinity. Really, the word used here was *Elohim*, which is plural, gods, or more accurately, "great ones." This brings us to another truth: our species was created by an extraterrestrial race (possibly *ultraterrestrial*, meaning from a different dimensional universe entirely).

Speaking of these extra- and ultraterrestrials, during my recent downtime, I have been watching the news. The world is going crazy, true, but hasn't it always been? So what is different? The difference is that now we number in the billions, and we are experiencing it all as one collective. Modern communications allow us to share events in real time. A hundred years ago, if an earthquake struck Japan, people in New York didn't know about it for days. But now we all watch it together and process it at the same time.

Have you ever heard of the Princeton EGG? This is the GCP or Global Consciousness Project. Researchers placed random number generators at random points around the globe. They noticed that when major world events happen, the generators stop being so random and start to sync up as if influenced by a large number of minds all focusing on the same thing. Go ahead. Look it up. It's fascinating. This reflects the Heisenberg, or uncertainty, principle, which I will discuss at length later. It was illustrated by the famous double-slit experiment, which quantum physicists stumbled upon while trying to determine if light was a wave or a particle. They decided to shine photons through two slits opposite a photosensitive cell. If it were a wave, they would get an interference pattern on the opposing cell. If it were a particle, they would see the two slits reflected in two lines of photons created as they passed through the slits as particles. They got an interference pattern and figured maybe the particles were somehow interfering with each other. So they cut it down to just one particle at a time. After a while, with only one photon particle passing through the slits, they still got an interference pattern! So what was interfering if there was just one photon? The answer is amazing. The particle was interfering with *itself*. It was in the superposition of going through one slit, both slits, and no slits all at the same time. It wasn't until it was *observed* that it seemed to make a decision and just choose one possibility. Basically, this principle shows us that reality is created when it is observed by a consciousness. (Also see Schrodinger's cat.)

Now imagine a world in which a collective consciousness of minds is observing the same major events at the same time. The results of the Princeton GCP reflect a change from random occurrence to synchronization, one that is reflected in our reality as indicated by the number generators. And imagine all those minds accepting, at the same time, the collective thought that the world is heading for some sort of major shift. And now might be a good time to mention the Schumann resonance, which has been called the heartbeat of the earth, the constant pulse of our electromagnetic field. It's a set of spectrum peaks in the extremely low frequency (ELF) portion of the planet's electromagnetic field spectrum. It's named after physicist Winfried Schumann who predicted it mathematically in 1952. After its discovery, the pulse was so constant that the US military used it to synchronize their clocks. However, since 1978, the Schumann resonance, the "heartbeat of the planet," has been steadily increasing, causing scientists to speculate this is a precursor to another impending flip of our magnetic poles. The Schumann resonance is believed to affect all life on earth, and some have speculated it can even affect our blood pressure. As you can imagine, this is of particular interest to me.

The world and the planet that it surrounds have always been in a state of flux. Change is the only constant, after all, and people have been predicting major shifts and "the end of days" since the beginning of days. But as I noted earlier, this period is unprecedented in how connected we all are. Now we are seeing a global pandemic, people are losing their sensibility, fighting the forces trying to protect them in the name of their "freedom"—freedom to do what? Spread and die of a plague? I don't want to turn this into a political treatise, but I do notice we are seeing more of the ultra/extraterrestrial presence in the mainstream media now. The US military and intelligence agencies are releasing more videos and documents on the subject of "UFOs" and more recordings of seemingly alien phenomena are popping up on social media, turning our collective consciousness to this topic. I mentioned my intense feeling that my time is growing short. I came for the show, and now the final act is beginning. I think this is my reason for rushing this message out now. So again, I apologize for the lack of structure in my writing. Something is happening, and it is sewn in the seeds of political, social, and spiritual disruption. We are drawing it to us.

Don't let the ignorant religious nuts tell you that all these emerging entities are demonic. They are not. They are largely like us—some are good, some are bad, and the majority are somewhere in between on the whole good/bad spectrum. Some are harmless and just like to fuck with us. The truly demonic never come to you directly. Sometimes they come to you as friends making promises but hiding knives.

The so-called right-wing "Christians" in the USA and elsewhere, these evangelicals, are fools and dupes and should not be harbored. They are already lost. They have lost Christ, and they have lost their damned minds. And that is all the time I will waste on them.

Back to Eden, shall we?

When the early humans first followed the serpent and began to understand lofty concepts like "good" and "evil," they figuratively ate from the tree of knowledge, represented in art and literature as that stupid apple. The Eden of Genesis is also said to have had a second tree, located in the center of the garden, the tree of life. Many scholars claim that these trees are one and the same. The tree of knowledge begets the tree of life—with knowledge comes eternal life, you see. I believe I once saw this tree, or a physical representation of it, while hiking in the hills of Northern Pennsylvania where I grew up. My friends and I were on acid at the time, and that tends to lend a profound meaning to everything you encounter. We went hiking in the wilderness around our small town as being in the woods seemed safer in that mental state than to be among "normal" people and "real" traffic. We would follow deer trails through the hills, and it was incredible. One day, we followed a deer trail and found this tree that was two trees that had grown together with a perfect arch between the two distinct trunks. Beyond that, you could not see where one tree ended and the other began. We called it the unitree and thought ourselves quite clever for coming up with that name, and we had felt it would be incredibly meaningful to walk under the arch formed by their uni-branch. And so, we did. I visited that tree many times in my younger years as it was a terrific spot to meditate. Sometimes, it was so still the tiny brush birds would flit over and literally sit on my shoulder and then flit away again as if testing to see if I were dangerous. I was not.

During my hikes into those rolling hills, I would come away feeling a deeper connection to Nature's God, the real God. As I said, God is a larger consciousness beyond time, and this text is a larger picture of that so be patient. Here is a fun anecdote I still enjoy telling my students about my own college days.

One weekend at our university, there was going to be a Laser Floyd Show. You know, a laser light show set to the music of Pink Floyd. As it so happened, the Grateful Dead had recently passed through the area, so everyone was holding something, mostly weed, but some of us had procured magic mushrooms as well. All my friends planned to eat their mushrooms and go to the Laser Floyd Show. At that point in my young life, I felt I lacked direction, and so I had made other plans. I wanted to try what Native Americans call a vision quest. My plan for that Saturday night was to hike up into the hills with some weed, mushrooms, and a blanket and camp by the unitree. There, I would wait for the universe to point me in some direction. At the time, I was living in a dormitory on campus, and my roommate was an irresponsible fellow who had lost his key to the dormitory. He suggested, since I would be camping in the hills all night, that I give him my key to the building so that he could get in after the Laser Floyd Show. I agreed, gave him my key, and set off with my blanket and drugs. I set up camp near the unitree, collected firewood, and started a small campfire. As the sun was setting, I ate my mushrooms and kicked back to smoke a bowl with my blanket wrapped around me. And I waited.

I don't know if you have ever seen a Pennsylvania sky at night when there are no electric lights around and it is real country dark, but there are more stars than I can even imagine, and I've seen it. You can see how it came to be called the Milky Way. I lay back to watch the light show. The mushrooms were kicking in hard, egged on by more weed, and I began to breathe deeply. My campfire was glowing coals and blue flame, and despite being alone in the forest at night with just a blanket and a wild imagination, I felt safe. I started singing to the stars. And then I noticed that there were fewer stars (was it because of my singing?). And I noticed that beyond the glowing coals of my fire, there was nothing but utter blackness. I kept my eyes on the sky and noticed that the few stars remaining were winking out, a few at a time. I figured out why when I felt the first drops of rain hit my face.

The next thing I knew, the sky had turned to blinding darkness and a torrential downpour. The coals of my small fire soon winked out like the stars above, and my blanket was heavy with water. I was soaked and sitting in a darkness so deep I couldn't see my hand in front of my face. I figured I had better try to find my way down the mountain. With my heavy waterlogged blanket still draped over me, I began to try to make my way back down the deer trail. I wandered off and felt pine needles slapping me in the face. I forgot the wise words of Douglas Adams, and I began to panic. I stumbled blind, altering my direction when the branches would hit my body. I stopped several times, just trying to get my bearings, before continuing again, and still, the rain came down. I must have wandered in the total darkness like this for an hour before I felt the ground inclining beneath my feet and figured that must mean I was heading down. Down was where I wanted to go. Soon I saw the lights of a town below through the trees, but I had no idea which side of the mountain I was on. Was it my town or the next town over? It didn't matter. It was light, it was civilization, so I headed for it. I slid down the side of the mountain, pricker bushes tearing at the legs of my jeans, tree branches scratching at my face, trying to protect myself with a sopping wet blanket that felt like it weighed a hundred pounds. I slid down through the rocky mud for what felt like an hour and finally landed in icy cold water up to my shins. I was standing in a little creek that ran beside a road. There was a streetlight several yards away, and I followed it back to civilization. I had come out near the university reservoir. A friend of mine lived nearby, so I walked to his house, but the lights were off. I had no idea what time it was. I sat on his porch until the rain eased up, and then I left my watery blanket on the porch and started walking up the road toward the university. All I wanted now was to get out of my wet clothes and into a hot shower. But I had no key to get into the dormitory, and I had no idea what time it was. I had no concept of the time. Hallucinogens will do that to you. I just knew it was late at night, but how late? I walked up to campus, past the college radio station where I worked. The glass door to get inside was locked, but I could see the clock on the wall opposite it—the clock that had been broken since I started working there. No help. But if this door was locked, then the dorms were probably still locked. Keep in mind, this is in the days before cellular phones, and I've never worn a watch. I also never thought to check the weather report before setting out on a camping trip with just a blanket, but such was I in college.

As I wandered along the campus sidewalk, wondering how I could get back into my dorm room, I wandered past the Methodist Church—the very church my mother had forced my sister and me to attend as children. I looked up at the bell tower and said silently, "All right, God, I went looking for the meaning of life, for some sense of direction, but now I just want to know what time it is!" And I hung my scratched, exhausted head, and there in the street, lying by my foot, was a Timex digital watch with the correct time. It was 3:14 a.m.

I tell you this story because it illustrates something that I have come to believe with all my heart: if you listen, the universe, God, speaks to you. And it also listens. I started to laugh. I thought it was hilarious. It was like God saying to me, "Well, you didn't win the big prize, but nobody goes home empty-handed!" And I kept that watch for many years after that, and I called it my booby prize. I no longer have it. I lost it when a friend of mine and I tried running away to California. It's sad that we sometimes lose such meaningful things to the ebb and flow of time and life. I never wore the watch. I still don't wear a watch. But I frequently check the time on my cell phone— and the weather forecast. Of course, when I relate this story to my students, I omit the bit about the drugs.

What was I telling you about? Ah, yes. The meaning of life and how to survive death.

CHAPTER 3

Immortality

All religions seem to promise eternal life. Yet do they deliver on this promise? They do if you can get to the truth those religions hide from you. True Christianity, the teachings of the true Christ, certainly does. But the religion that passes as Christianity today does not. Yeshua was not the first Christ, and he won't be the last. Christ was not his family name, of course. "Christ" is a title, same as "Buddha" or "Teacher." It means "Anointed One." Before Yeshua, there was John the Baptist, who anointed, or initiated, Yeshua. And before John the Baptist, there was Melchizedek. Hebrews 5:6 tells us that Yeshua was a priest in the order of Melchizedek. But there have been many Christs, many Buddhas. It is a consciousness. And when we talk about the Second Coming of Christ, we don't necessarily mean that Yeshua of Nazareth will return in a cloud with a multitude of trumpeting angels. We simply mean the Christ consciousness will return with new lessons for humanity.

But let's explore a bit more, just for the sake of absolute confusion. There are a few biblical scholars who claim that Yeshua had some connection to a Jewish sect known as the Essenes, and there is evidence to suggest that they are the ones who wrote the Nag Hammadi and the Dead Sea texts. The Essenes were said to have been known as the poor because they were minimalists, some historians claiming their only possessions were said to be an apron for covering their naughty bits and a trowel for digging holes to poop in. Laugh as you may, but the apron and the trowel are still carried in the rituals of Freemasonry. Freemasonry carries a lot of the surviving hidden truths that mainstream religion would rather be buried and forgotten. Will the Vatican ever open its vast library of hidden texts? Don't hold your breath. And the Masons will not share anything with you unless you are an initiate, and even then, only what you have earned via the degrees. But at least they will share under the right conditions.

The Essenes may not have been so poor, but they did live a communal lifestyle and share their possessions without the concept of ownership. Whether Yeshua was an Essene or merely was influenced by their beliefs, it is interesting to consider the educational practices of this sect. The Essenes were said to send their young boys away to be taught in what were called the Eastern mystery schools. If Mary and Joseph had been Essenes, this would account for the missing time in Yeshua's life between the Nativity and when he turned up arguing with the rabbis in the temple. Yeshua's core teachings were definitely in line with those of the Essenes, and this may come as a shock to some among us, but Yeshua was a liberal. Also, there are texts from one of these Eastern mystery schools, a Hindu school, at the time that record the arrival of a young student named Yeshua. He was said to have been a particularly bright student, but he angered the Brahmin by breaking the caste system. Young Yeshua, it seemed, insisted on hanging out with the Sudra—the peasant class. Guess who some of his friends were? Carpenters. It would seem young Yeshua learned a skill beneath his academic learnings, and this was such an offense that there was talk of killing the boy as an example. To protect him, some of his friends, fellow students, and/or teachers smuggled him out of the school and hid him away in a Buddhist temple. It was in these mystery schools that Yeshua learned about reincarnation. He taught this later in his life. When Yeshua spoke of being "born again," he was speaking quite literally. Regrettably, the church removed it from the scriptures. After all, how could they threaten you with eternal damnation if you knew you could just reincarnate?

A quick comment on reincarnation: it happens. You can find several well-documented accounts online with a simple search. There's the story of Joanna and Jacqueline Pollock, two little girls who were killed by a vindictive driver in Hexham, England, in 1957. Over a year later, their mother gave birth to twin girls whom they named Gillian and Jennifer. The two girls exhibited similar traits to their previous forms and even requested specific favorite toys that they recalled and to visit the same playground that was a favorite of the previous girls although by now their parents had relocated to Whitley Bay, east of Hexham. I won't go into the striking details. You can easily find them for yourself.

There is also an account of a girl who was born in a village in India. She recalled her past life with such detail that her family was able to track down her former family in another village. The girl was able to name each member of her previous family, share memories she had had of her time as their matriarch, and was even able to find the place where she had carved her former name into the frame of a doorway in the home. Children have recalled names, places, events, even languages that no one in their current family speaks. Most people come into this world with memories of past lives, but they quickly sink into the murky mists of the subconscious, only appearing in the conscious mind in the form of phobias, fantasies, or reoccurring dreams. When I was a child, I had trouble sleeping at night. I always felt there was someone watching me through my window (I sometimes even heard strange sounds outside, like heavy footsteps slowly walking up and down). I would play dead to fall asleep, thinking if I looked like I was dead, the presence outside would leave me alone. My mother would sit in my room with me and read her Bible until I fell asleep. She said she knew I was sound asleep when my bed would shake. This was because I had a reoccurring dream in which I was climbing up a trellis. Near the top, one of the thin wooden boards would break off in my hand, and I would fall backward, and when I hit the ground, the impact would cause my body to shake my bed. Sometimes I woke up on impact; other times, I went into a deep sleep.

Stories of children recalling memories of past lives seem to be on the rise, including a story I saw recently that was posted to the social media platform TikTok by a woman named Frederica Severinsen. When she told her four-year-old daughter that her friend was having a baby that would be named Esther, her daughter replied, "Oh, I know an Esther Mervin, but she lives really far away, and she's in prison." An odd thing for a four-year-old to say, to be sure, especially when their family as yet had no acquaintances named Esther. The mother checked the details of her daughter's story and found an Esther Mervin on an ancestry website, who had indeed lived "far away" (in America; Severinsen lives in the United Kingdom), and indeed, Esther had been in prison in the early 1900s. There is also the incredible story of James Leininger, a young boy who had detailed memories of being a pilot in the Pacific Theater during World War II. He had died when his plane was shot down by the Japanese and resulted in him having reoccurring nightmares that caused him to wake up, screaming, "Plane on fire! Little man can't get out!" He recalled the name of his carrier and other crew members that were still alive and had a remarkable knowledge of WWII-era military aircraft.

So yes, do a little research, and you will find that reincarnation happens, and it has likely happened to you. A quick note of warning: if you decide to go to a "regression therapy" hypnotist or anything like that, be wary of false memory or implanted memory tactics. Too many of these therapists are so desperate to prove the authenticity of their work that they will feed you misleading information. Be skeptical and do your due diligence to know the signs of suggestions of false memories.

What was I babbling about? Ah, yes. Yeshua and Christianity's Buddhist roots. Famed French anthropologist and ethnologist Claude Levi-Strauss wrote in his book *Tristes Tropiques* that, in fact, Buddhism and Christianity are sister religions. At least they were until the Crusades in the Dark Ages turned Christianity militant. Christ would never condone murdering people who do not share your views. Indeed, Yeshua may have adopted a lot of his teachings from an Eastern education. It takes many lifetimes to learn the real lessons of life. Life is a school, remember, and there are many grades. These pseudo-Christians today who think being born again just means deciding to devote your life to the dogma of the church have no idea. And Buddhism is not really so much a religion as it is a philosophy. True Buddhists do not proselytize, and they do not worship Buddha as a god, only revere him as a teacher.

Speaking of the damage done to the teachings of Christ by the dogma of the dim, it may trouble some of the more devout to know that Yeshua was married. He had a full beard and is referred to by the Jewish priests as "Rabbi." According to Rabbinic Law at the time, no man who was unmarried could be called "Rabbi." A beard also indicated that one had taken a wife. According to my (admittedly limited) understanding, Mary Magdalene was the wife of Yeshua, and she was no prostitute. She was actually a descendant of the house of Benjamin, a member of a well-respected family. As Yeshua was of the house of David, their union would have practically made them royalty. Both lineages were said to be descended from kings (hence the "King of the Jews" jokes). They had at least one child, a daughter they named Sarah. It is likely they also had at least one other child, a son, as it was considered a rabbi's duty under the "go forth and multiply" clause to father both a son and a daughter. After that, the duty to marry ended. The church demoted and shamed Mary Magdalene because a big part of their control of the new religion reflected a misogynistic need to subjugate and control women.

Heresy? Try this on for size: What if Yeshua was never crucified? Interestingly, crucifixion was not the prescribed punishment for his crimes. Yeshua was charged with heresy himself, which at the time was usually punished by stoning, not crucifixion. However, considering the deep anger he had roused in the community, let's assume that they figured, well, we're already crucifying these two thieves today, we'll just put Yeshua up next to them and call it a day. The tale I have been told is that the crucifixion was a deception, one that had been orchestrated under the guidance of John the Baptist.

This heretical account claims that Judas was in on it, and he kissed the wrong guy, setting up a patsy to be arrested by the Romans. The thirty pieces of silver Judas was paid for this betrayal was donated to the patsy's starving family. The patsy's name was Simon (not the apostle Simon, a different Simon). This is why, in the stations of the cross, the third time Yeshua stumbles on his way to Calvary, his cross is "taken up" by a man named Simon. Poor Simon took up a lot more than the cross that day in front of Pilate's house. The plan was to fake a resurrection by having Yeshua turn up with a superficial wound in his side to represent where the Centurion, Gaius Cassius Longinus, had jabbed Simon with his spear. Word would of course spread like wildfire that Yeshua had indeed returned from the dead. No one had a photograph of Yeshua or Simon, of course, to do a face-to-face comparison. People just knew of Yeshua and of what had happened to him, and they had the apostles all vouching for the authenticity of the story (with the possible exception of Judas who may have had a guilty conscience for his role in all this). This was all done with the intention of seeing the Christ's teachings carry on for thousands of years, and they have, except they have been overshadowed and hidden by the current religious power structure.

The account is fuzzy, admittedly. After all, hadn't Christ healed the severed ear of one of the arresting soldiers? Wouldn't that have identified Yeshua? And what of the piercing of his side by Gaius Cassius Longinus? Didn't that give us the Spear of Destiny, a relic so empowered by having been stained by Christ's blood that Hitler seized it when he marched into Austria where it was held in a museum? That, incidentally, is a fascinating story. I recommend the book *The Spear of Destiny* by Trevor Ravenscroft for a very detailed account of this holy relic. Again, all this is conjecture meant to establish a hidden tale decipherable by symbolism. The wounded ear of the Roman soldier symbolizes a mishearing of facts, his ear was wounded by false words when another man was misidentified as Yeshua, and the story of the Spear of Destiny, the blood flowing from Yeshua that was caught in a cup by Joseph of Arimathea, is symbolic of the continuation of the bloodline of Christ (his children by Mary Magdalene). Leonardo da Vinci hated the church, and although they were his biggest customers, always commissioning religious works from him, he often hid anti-church symbols in these same works. If you take a look at *The Last Supper*, you will notice that there is not a single cup on the table. This was da Vinci's way of saying that the Holy Grail is not a physical cup. Indeed, if you look at the Latin for "Holy Grail," you get *san greal*. Move the "g" in *greal* to the end of *san*, and you get *sang real*—royal blood.

According to this account, after the resurrection, Yeshua, Mary, and their children left Jerusalem as it was too hot to hang around, and they sailed to Gaul, or what is now the south of France. Interestingly, in this region, there came to be a group of devout Christians—real Christians, not those dogma-spewing evangelicals I continually attack—called the Cathars (or the Cathari, from the Greek, *Katharoi*, or "pure ones"). From the website Ancient.eu:

> Cathars rejected the teachings of the Catholic Church as immoral and most of the books of the Bible as inspired by Satan. They criticized the Church heavily for the hypocrisy, greed, and lechery of its clergy, and the Church's acquisition of land and wealth. Not surprisingly, the Cathars were condemned as heretical by the Catholic Church and massacred in the Albigensian Crusade (1209–1229 CE) which also devastated the towns, cities, and culture of southern France.

The "massacre" consisted of the Cathars running down the mountain from their stronghold and throwing themselves into bonfires set by the forces of the Catholic Church. They self-immolated rather than be forced into submission, and some say they did this as a distraction to buy some time for members of their group to smuggle something sacred down the cliffs to a waiting ship. What could this have been? Direct descendants of Yeshua's bloodline? Your guess is as good as mine.

There is a painting by Nicolas Poussin dating from 1637–38 that depicts a tomb in the Gaul region of the south of France. It is entitled *Et in Arcadia ego*, "And in Arcadia Am I." This mysterious painting and the symbolism contained within it are worth the attention of one far more schooled in the language of fine art than I, but it is loaded with sacred geometry, which would indicate it is sharing a subtle yet powerful message.

I do not mean to detract from the image of Yeshua as an enlightened spiritual entity. These histories are over two thousand years old.

Historical records from that time are not exactly unimpeachable, and for every scholarly paper held up as truth, there are hundreds of others that question it or outright contradict it. Whatever Yeshua was, an enlightened teacher but a man nonetheless or an entity from a higher frequency capable of performing the miracles attributed to him, the bottom line is that he was a great and enlightened being. Was he the genuine prophesied Messiah? Was he indeed the Son of God, created through Immaculate Conception? As a collective species, we can't even agree on that. Although there is the prophecy that said when the Messiah dies, no bone of his body shall be broken. In crucifixion, the cause of death is suffocation as the weight of the body slowly stretches the lungs so as to make breathing impossible. If the condemned took too long to die, the Romans would break the legs to expedite the process. Yeshua hung on his cross for about six hours, so there was no need to break his legs (they did, as noted earlier, jab him with a spear), and he is said to have perished with no broken bones, which would fulfill this prophecy. Also, if he had hung on the cross for only six hours, there is a chance that he may have even survived the crucifixion. A few days' rest in a cave and he might have been up on his feet again with no need of a patsy to take his place. The point is, we don't know, and as history grows more distant, we will likely never know. There is a rumor in some military circles that extraterrestrials presented a holographic recording of the actual crucifixion of Christ to top people in the intelligence community, but again... who the hell knows? If anyone does, they aren't talking. And if they are, they are being shouted down by those with conflicting agendas and more powerful voices.

Either way, the legend, the message, and the symbolism live on, and you can do your own research and choose your own adventure. Isn't that fun? No matter which tale you choose to believe, back up your choice with sound research and never let them tell you this is "conspiracy theory." I hate that expression as it has been turned to be synonymous with "bullshit." That's so Orwellian it sickens me. Sure, in these days of "fake news" and "alternative facts," the infosphere is full of damaging and ridiculous conspiracy theories, but look for the mark of time. Look for supportive evidence. Conspiracies happen.

Every major turning point in human history is marked with them. As the character Hunter Gathers said in what could very well be my favorite animated series *The Venture Brothers*, "The minute God crapped out the third caveman a conspiracy was hatched against one of them!"

Whatever else he may have been, Yeshua was what the Buddhists call a *Boddhisatva*. A Boddhisatva, if you don't know, is a soul that has mastered the lessons of life, but rather than moving on to the higher frequencies chooses to become a teacher on this frequency to help others to advance. The Boddhisatva will say that they will not move on until every soul is enlightened, down to every blade of grass. I cannot think of a more noble dedication. And for that, I personally am happy to claim Yeshua the Christ as my personal Lord and Savior. I don't know what he really was, and lord knows the church has done everything they can to hide his real story, from the deletion of many of his teachings in the apocryphal texts to their misogynistic mistreatment of the memory of Mary Magdalene. Who can we trust? Only the soul himself, and the universal consciousness for whom he may have spoken. We certainly can't trust the pagan emperor Constantine who began this great cover-up to preserve his empire, setting in motion the muddying of the historical waters over the course of the next 1,696 years. That has done far more to diminish the effect of the Christ on this frequency than anything.

What do I mean by "frequencies?" The short answer is that I mean the different wavelengths that hide different worlds from our physical senses. Yeshua knew of this when he said that heaven is not above or below us but all around us—"it is in our midst" (Luke 17:20). We'll get to that later. For now, let's continue talking about Yeshua and true eternal life through reincarnation.

You have likely reincarnated before. This is to say, you have been born again, and again, which means you have died before. You likely just can't recall the experience. It's pretty heavy, and we tend to drop the heavy things. The trick to eternal life is to gain the ability to maintain your consciousness, to keep your soul intact, through the process of death and rebirth. These physical bodies are just meant to be temporary molds, like a cast helping a broken bone to maintain its proper shape until it is healed. These physical bodies age over time. To put it less delicately, they rot like fruit. If you choose to marry, be sure you marry someone that you enjoy talking to, someone who can make you laugh and keep the conversation interesting because that hotness? That fades away damn quick. They shrivel up like an old apple. And don't you dare get turned off by this because your ass is shriveling too. This is the cause of far too many unhappy marriages and divorces, broken families, and resulting social decay. Don't marry just for the physical appearance or because the sex is good. Marry for the conversation and the memories you share.

I'm not writing a self-help book on marriage, though. That death thing, that is scary. And it's only scary because most of us have no idea what it is. We just know it is something completely different, something permanent, something so intense that we stop being who we are. We leave our bodies and everything! Well, your body isn't you, so relax. "What happens when we die? I'm so scared!" Well, what happens when you change your outfit? I don't mean to trivialize this. Death is a much bigger deal than changing your sweatpants, but the concept is not so different. The trick is remembering who you are when you see yourself in a new pair of sweatpants.

This is what I was talking about when I said *integrity* is key. I'm going to do the unthinkable here, the one thing you should never do in a speech. Watch this.

Webster's Dictionary defines *integrity* as (1) firm adherence to a code of especially moral or artistic values: *incorruptibility*; (2) an unimpaired condition: *soundness*; (3) the quality or state of being complete or undivided: *completeness*.

For definition 1, see the Two Rules of life back in chapter 1. Here, we are concerned more with definitions 2 and 3. This is developing the learned ability to maintain an unimpaired condition, staying complete or undivided, when you shuffle off this mortal coil (i.e., shed your skin). Lose your flesh. Dump the husk and move beyond your limited physical senses.

You see, these meat suits we wear limit our perception. Our eyes can only see a small portion of the complete light spectrum. Our physical eyes can only see good ol' Roy G. Biv, if you recall your third-grade science. Everything that reflects light above the infrared or below the ultraviolet is invisible to us. In fact, you never actually really "see" anything in your physical state. Everything is piped into where you are locked safely away in your little bone bubble, your skull. You are contained in a mushy hard drive of tissue and neurons, the brain. You're a brain in a jar. Your only view of the world is what your instruments can detect. It's as though you were a frightened little person hiding in a tiny concrete panic room, and all you could see or hear from the outside world was what was fed in through your external cameras and microphones. And if you know your heist films, you know that these can easily be deceived. There is much, much, much more out there. In the corporeal state, in these bodies, the vast majority of it is invisible and largely undetectable to the average person. Physicists are working some of it out, but they are not average people.

When your physical body ceases to function and it can no longer contain you, you find yourself in the real world unfiltered. It is overwhelming, and yes, it can be scary at first. You are adrift in a sea of frequencies, and you have to know how to tune into the one you want. This is why my advice on facing death is to embrace it with a sense of joy and laughter. I know, this sounds idiotic, but hear me out. If you go into that sea of frequencies, you tune in to what you feel. It's all about emotion. Death is one tremendous emotional release, a blinding white flash of emotion. (It's great—it's *so* bright it would hurt your eyes to look at it, but luckily, you don't have eyes anymore.) If you feel joy and love at that moment, the transition is much more pleasant. If you go in feeling fear or anger, you do not tune into the good or higher frequencies ("heaven") so easily. Why do you think it is that most ghosts wandering the earth are echoes of people who died in fear or sorrow or anger, the lower energies? It's always the suicides and murder victims, isn't it? They didn't tune in to the higher frequencies fast enough, and they left an imprint on this world.

What's that? You don't believe in ghosts? That's fine. You don't have to. You've probably just never seen one. They do exist, however. They don't need your belief to do that. I have seen ghosts in this life, on more than one occasion. Maybe I will tell you about them later if this book needs some padding. I do not profess to know exactly what ghosts are, if they are indeed the disembodied consciousness or just a sort of reflection, imprint, or echo left on this frequency by a strong emotion. Many ghosts follow repetitive patterns such as walking down the same staircase or searching through the same closet, which makes me think they may, at least some of them, just be echoes. I have seen them, and I have communicated with what I believe may have been ghosts on a Ouija board. Incidentally, do *not* play with these things, and do not let your children play with them. Ninety-eight percent of the time, they are just a dull parlor game, something to try to trick your friends with at sleepovers and give yourselves the heebie-jeebies. But there is that 2 percent of serious danger from some not-so-nice entities. Ask around. I'm sure you know a few people who have a story. Again, if the book needs padding, I will tell you some of mine later.

So you've died and you forgot to go out with love and joy, and now the full flood of frequencies is overwhelming. Honestly, it will be overwhelming even if you go out with love and joy. It is hard to be happy when you die. It's hard not to be afraid because many of us die in terrifying ways. But when you feel yourself going, accept it. Embrace it. Laugh with it if you can. Think of all the fun you've had and how much more fun you're going to have when you see all those loving consciousnesses again. You are caught in the undertow of the tremendous emotional energy, and you are being washed away to oblivion. What do you do?

The Native Americans use the analogy of a great body of water. In physical life, we are all individual droplets taken from the Great Lake. As the raindrops return to the sea, so must we return to that Great Lake. There, we are no longer individual droplets. Our identity as an individual is reabsorbed into the greater body of water, and we are indiscernible from it. This is death of identity, or ego, not of consciousness. Consciousness is energy and therefore cannot be destroyed. It can only change. Still, this is what you want to avoid if you want to achieve eternal life. It's not unpleasant. You just cease to exist as your own individual consciousness. You become one with the collective consciousness again, the universal mind, or God. Call it what you will. I like the Native analogy, but I had it explained to me using something more solid. I was told to imagine that I am a minted coin. I have distinctive markings, a symbol, a date, a motto, etc. But if I am dropped into a vat of molten metal, I begin to melt and become one with that glowing hot vat of goo. If I am scooped out soon enough and allowed to cool, some of my original markings may remain, a little of my former self can still be seen. These are past-life memories.

So how do we retain all these memories, these markings, of our past lives? How do we keep our consciousness from becoming reabsorbed into the collective? This is where that integrity comes in. If you have already mastered the life-and-death process, you'll be fine. It will all be familiar to you when you cross over into the larger world, and you can hang out there and decide what you want to do next. If you are new to this and you haven't yet built up any integrity, then you will be absorbed faster, and you need to defend against this.

If you want to. As I said, becoming one with the collective and losing your individual identity is not altogether unpleasant, but you, as you know yourself, will cease to exist. You will become part of the larger consciousness. You will know everything—and nothing. You will be everything—and nothing.

So how do you build up integrity? You use a *mandala*. I like that word because it comes from Buddhism, but some people call it a *sigil*, a *token*, or an *icon*. It has many names in many languages. There are websites that can show you how to create your sigil, but it is just a symbol that is unique to you. It represents you as a consciousness, a soul, your true self. It must be uniquely yours, of you, created by you. You can't use other known symbols, so no football team logos or rock band insignia. It must be only yours so that you don't confuse yourself with another, and no other will confuse themselves with you (this causes multiple personality disorder when more than one consciousness reincarnates to the same physical form). Once you have created your sigil, as Gandalf said, "Keep it secret! Keep it safe!" Share it with no one, not even your true love or your pets. Don't tattoo it on your shoulder or paint it on your walls. You can draw it on paper to create it, but once it is committed to memory, destroy the physical form. It should only exist in your mind. For this reason, it is a good idea to start with a simple design, something easy to recall. You can add to it as you grow your soul through future lives. Here's an example of a simple sigil:

There you go. It's not impressive, but I do think it is original. I don't think I have seen one like it before. And it is simple so that a beginner can remember it easily and recall a mental image of it in the mind whenever needed. Depending on your ability, you may choose a slightly more complex design. Be creative, but make sure you can recall every detail. The intricate mandalas produced by Buddhists are those of ascended masters, so they are very complex. For now, keep it simple. As I said, there are websites and books that can give you better sigil-making strategies, but the main point is the same: make sure it is original and from you, make sure you can recall every detail, and make sure you keep it secret. This is your new name, and anyone who studies magic will tell you to protect your name at all costs. You know those movies in which people conjure spirits, demons, or entities by drawing symbols? They are using the symbol to control that entity. It's the same idea. The symbol is the true name of the entity.

Once you have a sigil, meditate on it frequently. Connect all your memories, experiences, and joyful emotions to it. I recommend the barrel-of-monkeys method to begin. If you know the game of barrel-of-monkeys, it is a little plastic barrel full of little plastic monkeys with linkable arms. The idea is to build a chain of monkeys starting with one monkey, and then dipping it into the barrel to link up another monkey, and then lowering the chain of two monkeys down to pick up a third, and so on, making the chain longer all while keeping your hold on the first monkey. Do this with memories. Link one big, important emotionally charged memory to your sigil, and then link others to that memory, and so on. Make a frequent habit of meditating, holding a clear image of your sigil in your mind. Connect it to as many of your memories and experiences as you can. After all, that is all life is in the end—memories and experiences. That is all you are, really, and that's all you take with you when you die.

When you feel yourself dying, or find yourself dead, throw that sigil up like a shield. Use it to keep all your memories and experiences—*you*—connected. Don't let the rush of emotion overwhelm you. Cling to that sigil like a life raft in a stormy sea. Calm your mind, focus on your sigil, and follow the guides to a newly reincarnated form. If your integrity is not yet strong and you find yourself fading into the ether, becoming one with the collective, losing your sigil, you may not have time to pick the ideal life. Slide into the first one that opens. Sure, you may have spent this life as a rather well-to-do first-world socialite, but don't shy away from being born again as a poor third-world dirt farmer. It builds character. And what is character? That's right: *integrity*. In the long run, you will develop into a fully conscious, fully secured sentient being that can exist wherever and however it sees fit. What's one life? We all have our bad days at school. And you choose what to do with every life you are given. You make it your own, and if you recall things from a past life, the new life is easier. Keep in mind, however, that you will not recall much your first time around. You have to build. Don't lose yourself in your new life. All those magical things we knew as babies and forgot? Try not to forget. Keep your sigil in your conscious mind. Don't let it slip into the subconscious. Be a meditative baby! What else do you have to do? Recall as much as you can. At first, it may not be much. It may manifest as a reoccurring dream, a mental picture of a house or a building, an artistic work, a place, bits of a song or a language, a combination of colors. Smells—remember smells. They are a powerful trigger for memory. This is why it is a good idea to burn incense when you meditate. Hang on to all the memories. The more you reincarnate, the easier it gets. The things that are held the deepest by you, the emotions and beliefs and experiences that truly define you, these are the things that are easiest to recall. Bind them together. This is what the sigil is for.

I use the word "recall" more than the word "remember." You remember everything. It's all stored in the subconscious and in what is known as your Akashic Record. But you won't be able to *recall* it to your conscious mind. It will be forgotten, but like all data, it does not mean it can't be recovered.

I used the word *magic* a few paragraphs back. I know that makes some of you consider me a fool, and others, a charlatan. Keep in mind as we continue that what we consider science today was seen as magic to our forebearers. For those who take the so-called scientific approach to death and believe that consciousness is just a chemical reaction in the brain and that when the brain dies the consciousness dies with it, I say you're showing your lack of imagination. Do you have data stored on a hard drive? How about a cloud? What happens when your laptop dies? Is that data gone forever? Your brain is the hard drive. You are the data. Back yourself up, sunshine. Ever heard the old joke about Jesus and Satan at their computers? Jesus never loses his documents because Jesus saves! Okay, it's a dumb joke, but that's all I have for you here. Science has become like a religion unto itself in that it has lost its true meaning to dogma. New ideas that fly in the face of ancient beliefs will get you excommunicated, and your funding will be cut off. So sure, faster-than-light travel isn't possible, right? Jackasses. And yeah, I know, in religion, it's the ancient ideas that get lost to the new dogma, but are there not ancient scientific ideas that have been lost to the new scientific dogma? Have you ever looked at some of the crazy things described in those ancient cuneiform tablets from Mesopotamia? There was a much more advanced civilization with a much different and more developed science on this planet long before ours arose from their dust. The world of archaeology is full of leftover tidbits that the current dogma can't and won't try to explain. How was our species created in the first place? Why are we so much more advanced than the other species that got roughly the same start we did? How did primitive cultures learn about the order of our solar system? How did ancient civilizations know to build the Great Pyramid? Let's begin with that one in the next chapter.

CHAPTER 4

Ancient and Antediluvian Civilizations

I don't expect I am going to spend a lot of time on this chapter as I am no archaeologist, and all the information I am going to share with you here is readily available from other sources. Also, if you are reading this book, then you likely have a mind that pursues such interests and you are already aware of all the peculiar and little-known facts about the Pyramid. Let's begin with a question: How many sides does the Great Pyramid at Giza have? If you said four, then you are wrong. If you said five, you are showing some ingenuity by counting the base. However, if you said nine, counting the base, you would be correct. The four sides of the Great Pyramid are evenly split from base to tip by very subtle indentations. These angles are barely noticeable and can best be seen as the sun is low in the sky, casting shadows along the stones. These angles can be clearly seen twice a year, on the equinoxes. Each of the angles aligns perfectly with one of the four cardinal directions.

Many historians and laypeople believe that the mystery of how the Great Pyramid was built has been solved. They are misinformed. There are many theories, some of them with more credentialed support than others, but none of these theories explains all the incredible details involved in the construction, location, dimensions, and design of this incredible structure. There is a fascinating documentary available on YouTube called "The Revelation of the Pyramids." I would recommend giving that a watch to learn more of the stunning details regarding the purpose and intent behind its construction. It was not a tomb. That is common knowledge today. The blocks of the pyramids are so perfectly fitted, and in many places without the use of mortar, that a razor blade could not fit between them. There are several curved blocks, and blocks cut with irregular edges, that fit perfectly with the blocks supporting them. Stone working areas near the pyramids show signs of mechanical tool cuts dating back to 2750 BC.

Nothing is random in the Great Pyramid's structure, and there is constant harmony in its measurements and dimensions. The visible height divided by two gives the height of the chevron summit of the upper chamber. Divide it by three, you get the height of the upper chamber's ceiling; by four, the chevron summit of the middle chamber; by five, the floor in the lowest chamber; and by seven, the floor in the middle chamber. Even more significant, the height of the Pyramid's largest visible surface, the four concave faces, divided by the base, equals *pi*, 3.141. Curiously, the "sarcophagus" found in what has been named "The King's Chamber" never held a mummified corpse, but its dimensions perfectly match those of the ark of the covenant. If you know your Old Testament, you know that the ark carried a powerful electrical charge. It is even recorded to have electrocuted servants that got too close to it. When an Israelite named Uzzah touched it, he was "struck down by God." This God was likely in the form of ten thousand volts as the ark's description matches that of a giant capacitor. This is remarkable when we learn the schematics and original purpose of the Great Pyramid were that of a power generator.

Stranger still, the Great Pyramid was built at the precise mathematical center of planet Earth. It aligns perfectly along a twenty-five-thousand-mile-long circular loop around the globe with other ancient mystery sites as Easter Island to the Nazca Lines in Peru, Machu Picchu, Cuzco, Sacsayhuaman, and the site of the Paratoari Pyramids. In Africa, it passes directly through the lands of the Dogon Tribe, an ancient people who knew about the orbits of the planets of our solar system and the Sirius stars B and C long before modern astronomers mapped them. It then passes through the Tassili N'Ajjer

in Algeria. In Egypt, it goes through the Siwa Oasis and the temple
there, then through Giza, and then Petra in Jordan, Ur in Iraq where
Abraham was born, the structure of Persepolis in Iran, and Mohenjo
Daro in Pakistan. Then through Khajuraho in India, Pyay in Burma,
Sukhothai in Thailand, and Angkor Wat in Cambodia, all places
known to be dwelling places of gods. It crosses across many other
ancient and lost sites, and the really peculiar thing is that it aligns
with the Earth's original equator, before our planet was tilted on its
axis at 23.5 degrees. If you locate the North Pole of Earth based on
this original equator, you get a triangle that connects this point with
Giza and Nazca that precisely matches the Great Pyramid's ratio. The
distance between Nazca and Giza is the same as between Teotihuacan
and Giza. It is also the same between Angkor Wat and Nazca and
between Mohenjo Daro and Easter Island. And the distance from
Easter Island to Giza is 10,000 × *pi*. The distance between Angkor
Wat and Giza multiplied by pi equals the Giza-Nazca distance,
and the Giza-Nazca distance multiplied by pi gives us the Nazca-
Angkor Wat distance. And most of the sites that clearly mark this
ancient equator are mirror representations of stellar objects over the
Earth. For example, the Pyramids at Giza are a mirror of the Belt of
Orion. Many researchers believe that the suspected structures in the
Cydonia region on Mars serve the same purpose and mirror the Giza
Pyramids and the Sphinx. In fact, the meridian that passes through
the Great Pyramid divides the emerged lands into equal surfaces,
which makes Giza the central point of the planet. The Great Pyramid
is a geographic reflection of the Earth, a maquette of the northern
hemisphere that can be verified with calculations. And its dimension
is also the average distance run by point in one second on the equator by the Earth's rotation, meaning it tells anyone who knows how
to read it how fast the planet is spinning. I won't go into this much
more as I hate math (I know, right? The shame!), and I get the feeling
that if you are reading this, you are already aware of these facts. My
point is that the purpose of the Great Pyramid seems to be that of a
mathematical message and a marker: a marker to travelers approach-
ing from beyond Earth, and a message to civilizations that arise here.

So why did they bother to haul these gigantic granite blocks from a quarry five hundred miles away from the site of the Great Pyramid, blocks that weighed as much as two and a half tons? It was probably because the builders knew even then that granite doesn't change over time, its dimensions stay constant, and from dimensions we get numbers, and from numbers mathematics, a universal language that carries meaning and messages. For example, if you use a compass and the central point of the pyramid as seen from above, and you draw two circles—one inside the pyramid and the other outside—then subtract their lengths in meters, the result is the value of the speed of light in millions of meters per second. The speed of light in millions of meters per second is 299.79. The difference between the measurements is also 299.79. If you think all these numbers are coincidence, think about how hard it is to guess three winning lottery numbers.

All this is explained much better in the video I mentioned, "The Revelation of the Pyramids," which can be found on YouTube. In the video, the author describes being told several amazing and verifiable facts by an unnamed informant. All we know about this informant is that it took them thirty-seven years to research and collect the information presented. That the informant wishes to remain unidentified is not surprising as the government of Egypt, specifically the Ministry of Antiquities, is renowned for protecting secret information about Giza, discouraging and covering up new discoveries, and even arresting archaeologists who flaunt evidence that goes against their stated accepted histories. The perfect construction of the Great Pyramid, the perfect fit of the stones, the sheer weight and the mechanics it would take to move them, the mapping and the dimensions, all seem to indicate that there is much more to the history of this structure than most are told. If you've ever seen the television comedy series *The Big Bang Theory*, then you are familiar with the theme song performed by the band Barenaked Ladies. I like this song, but whenever I hear it, when they get to the part that says, "We built the Wall, we built the Pyramid!" I think, "No, we didn't!" If we did, why can't we do it today, even with all our modern technological advancements? If we built it, then do it again. Prove it. Prove it and silence the extra/ ultraterrestrial researchers like myself once and for all.

As the narrator for the video summarizes at the 1:22:50 mark,

> We could keep thinking that all we saw was just a matter of chance, that The Great Pyramid was indeed cap stoned, even if such construction were hardly possible in such little time, that if the Great Pyramid were signaling the equinoxes it was a matter of chance. If the Great Pyramid was featuring the pi number and the Golden Number, it was a matter of chance. That the cubit was picked by chance, that we could have accidentally built the only possible pyramid to bridge altogether the cubit, pi, the golden number, and the meter, and if those values were expressed in meters in the Great Pyramid, it was by chance. That if the most ancient constructions we visited where the most massive blocks were the best fitting, it was by chance. That if other people on Earth were using hieroglyphs, mummifying their dead, designing precise calendars, had great astronomical skills, and were building with the same antiseismic techniques [without cross-communication] or leaving any explanation, it was by chance. That if so many sacred sites were on a circle as long as our equator, it was by chance. That if some distance ratios were linked to the Golden Number, it was by chance. That if [the dimensions of the Great Pyramid] evened our planet's speed of rotation, it was by chance. That if the speed of light was indicated in the pyramid, it was still and always by chance, two hypotheses were then possible. Hypothesis A: We should rethink the sense of the word 'chance' because if it were working so many miracles, we'd better call

[it] God. I prefer hypothesis B: We could think that too many coincidences were hurting coincidences, that our history had missing links maybe as staggering as my informant's discoveries, and it was time to craft a rational explanation for the mysteries of our past.

My transcribing skills from the video are not great, and the narrator's accent really screws up the automated closed captioning, but I think her points are clear and correct. The video covers many other verifiable points regarding information coded into the Great Pyramid. The Pyramid itself was designed to withstand the tests of time. Even after some major cataclysm, such as nuclear holocaust, seismic instabilities, or an extinction-level event like an asteroid strike could wipe out our entire civilization, certain sturdy structures would still survive, even for centuries, but not for millennia. The Pyramid was constructed to do just that, so we can only assume the mathematics encoded within it is of utmost importance.

I am reminded of the problem of the Yucca Mountain Nuclear Waste depository. This is a site designated by the United States Department of Energy to store the bulk of the world's nuclear waste. The problem is, if our civilization is wiped out in the next, oh, 350,000 years, the large stockpile of nuclear waste will still just be sitting there, deadly as ever, for any future civilization—terrestrial or otherwise—to stumble upon. The problem is, how do we leave a warning to these future civilizations so that they will know not to unleash all that radioactive death? These future civilizations will not understand our languages or symbolism, so one promising solution is the universal language of mathematics. We may have to devise our own universal marker. The Great Pyramid seems to serve a similar purpose, but more to the point of the movement of our planet. It is a map and a calendar, and it indicates events that we should likely start to expect. The Sphynx, the apparent guardian of the Pyramid, also is said to harbor its own secrets. Did you know there is a large cube-shaped chamber beneath the Sphinx's paws? And there is some sort of large switch built behind the Sphinx's right ear. And there appears to be a manhole-like cover over an entrance at the top of the Sphinx's head. We still don't know what could be buried in the chamber or what the functions of the switch or entrance are because the Egyptian Ministry of Antiquities will not let anyone near it. And speaking of antiquities, the markings on the Sphynx indicate it was subjected to fluvial erosion (water) rather than aeolian erosion (wind). The last time there was enough water flowing through that region to cause these distinctive erosion marks was around seven thousand to nine thousand years ago when the ice from the last ice age was melting. The ice covered that region for twenty thousand years, which indicates the Sphynx may be roughly thirty thousand years old. Were early humans building structures of this magnitude that far back?

Aside from its myriad of mathematical messages, some researchers believe that the Great Pyramid also served a more utilitarian purpose, that of a massive power generator. The Pyramid was once protected by an outer casing comprised of 5.5 million tons of white tufa limestone, which would have given it a smooth appearance that shone white in the sunlight. White tufa limestone is unique in which it does not contain magnesium, which makes it an excellent insulator. Also, the granite used in the Pyramid's construction lines the narrow passageways inside. Granite contains high amounts of quartz crystal, making it a good conductor of piezoelectricity. The ionized air around the granite further increases its electroconductivity. And the capstone was made of gold. The capstone, of course, has long since disappeared. The limestone was also stripped away by later civilizations that were not aware of its earlier significance to be used as a building material for other structures. There are carved images of people holding what appear to be large light bulbs, and there are decorated chambers within the pyramid with no source of light, and yet there is no buildup of ash on the interior stone walls to indicate torches were ever lit inside. And there is the account of a scientist, Sir William Siemens, who stood at the summit of the Pyramid in the late 1800s and detected electricity still emanating from the structure itself. There are thousands of articles available that go into detail regarding how the Pyramid generated electricity. Many note the fact that a system of underground rivers runs beneath the Giza plateau. Geographers have shown that the Nile itself ran directly past the Pyramid over three thousand years ago. A theory that has gained a lot of attention in recent years claims that the Pyramid was built to harness the piezoelectrical properties of the waters of these rivers, allowing it to concentrate electromagnetic energy in its internal chambers. A study published in the *Journal of Applied Physics* in 2018 goes into great detail regarding the Pyramid's potential as a power generator. The paper is entitled "Electromagnetic Properties of the Great Pyramid: First Multipole Resonances and Energy Concentration" (Mikhail Balezin, Kseniia V. Baryshnikova, et. al.) and suggests, among other things, that the water from the rivers was drawn up into the narrow passages in the limestone of the Pyramid through capillary action. Similar to the concept of Tesla's design for his Wardenclyffe Tower, energy is thus drawn from the earth and projected skyward. This is also similar to the HAARP array in Gakona, Alaska, which directs energy to the ionosphere. If anyone out there still thinks the Pyramid is a tomb full of mummies…ugh.

I have spent far too much time discussing the Great Pyramid. It is obvious that I am fascinated by it. Sadly, I have never been to visit it. I have been to sacred sites in Nepal, China, Oman, Korea, Cambodia, Thailand. I've traveled to twenty-five countries so far… but still have not checked Egypt off my bucket list. Frankly, I don't have much of an urge to do so. Even if I went to Egypt, I'd never get close to these monuments, and friends who have been there tell me Cairo is not worth the trip. They said, "The image of Cairo in your mind is better than Cairo in real life." As I've said, all the information you need to learn about it is widely available. Just always remember to check your sources. The point is that it certainly seems to indicate the existence of ancient, advanced civilizations. I suspect many archaeologists are correct in their belief that the Pyramid, and the Sphinx are much older than the official estimates indicate.

The world is full of established oddities that do not fit into our accepted history. You can find out about hundreds, if not thousands of them, by checking out a book by archeologist Michael Cremo entitled *Forbidden Archeology*. It is quite the tome. Also, check out his online site of the same name for recent discoveries and developments.

Other ancient sites indicate ancient cities of advanced technological capabilities. The Richat Structure, or the Eye of the Sahara in North Africa, was the site of the city that is the basis for the legends of Atlantis. You can still see the five concentric rings that alternated from water to land as described in Plato's account of Atlantis.

I apologize, I am feeling particularly scatterbrained tonight, and I will probably have to break my rule of "swooping" and come back and do some serious editing to this chapter. All I am trying to express with this so far is that there is more than ample evidence that technologically advanced civilizations have been on this planet for eons. We are not the first, and we likely will not be the last. Our physical bodies still carry some of the DNA of the peoples that were here before us. Some of them did not originate here, and these include the ones that created us in our current form. You may have heard of them referred to as the Anunnaki or "those who from heaven to earth came." In the Bible, it describes angels descending from heaven "in flames." Sounds like rocket ships, doesn't it? And in the book of Ezekiel, Ezekiel describes the machines that he could only describe as wheels within wheels with eyes all around and the four "living" beings he witnessed. He was just some simple fellow with no understanding or ability to describe the advanced technology he was seeing. He tried, though, God bless him, and they apparently liked that because they took Ezekiel up. He's still up there, you know. He came back once before, I am told, but left again. He's not the only one. There are already millions of our species occupying other planets and dimensions. But I am getting ahead of myself. I will tell you all about this and the Veil later on. The Veil is what we call the perception of a partition between frequencies. It's wild. Civilizations exist all around us, right here on earth, but they are on the other side of the Veil. We interact with them sometimes and not always on purpose. Our religions, legends, and internet chat rooms are full of accounts of such encounters. Fortean researcher John Keel wrote about them extensively in his books *The Mothman Prophecies* and *Our Haunted Planet*. Fascinating stuff. If you haven't read them, I highly recommend doing so. Later on, I will tell you a story about my early forays into these other worlds when I was reading *The Mothman Prophecies*.

Oh hell, I need a break to rest my mind, so I'll tell you now. I was living in Pittsburgh, and that part of the United States—Western Pennsylvania and the Ohio River Valley—is a very active region for oddities. It is a weak spot in the Veil. The town of Kecksburg, just southeast of Pittsburgh, is famous for a UFO that crashed there in 1965. And West Virginia and the Ohio River Valley are where the events described in *The Mothman Prophecies* took place. So I was drawn to the research. Around midnight, I was awake in my apartment, reading this book. I was on chapter 9, entitled, "Wake Up Down There!" or something like that. This chapter describes strange phone calls the people of Point Pleasant, West Virginia, had been receiving during the strange events of 1967 that led up to the tragic collapse of the Silver Bridge on December 15. Some of the phone calls sounded like a man speaking very fast in some unidentifiable language—others were just a random series of beeps. As soon as I read that, my landline phone rang (we all still had landlines back then). So there I was, alone in my apartment at midnight, reading this creepy book, reading that particular bit about phone calls, and my phone rings. I was enthralled. I walked to the desk and picked up my cordless phone from the charger. I said "Hello?" into it. And of course, I heard a random series of beeps like I had never heard before. This was the age of dial-up internet, fax machines, and recorded voice mail, and I was familiar with all of them, and this was nothing like any of them. To this day, I still can't describe how I felt. As I listened, I wasn't so much frightened as I was fascinated. Between breaks in the odd beeps, I decided to try to have a conversation. "Oh, hi! You don't say! Well, sure, if you're gonna ask about the price of pumpernickel…" This went on for only about thirty seconds before the call disconnected. When I hung up the phone, my apartment felt very quiet, and that's when the fear set in. I slept with my light on for a few nights after that. I still sleep with my light on sometimes. By the way, the line about the price of pumpernickel I got from another book I read at that time, *Groucho and Me*, the autobiography of Groucho Marx. There's a chapter in that book entitled "What Price Pumpernickel?" in which Groucho talks about how he always gauged the strength of the economy by the price of pumpernickel bread.

What was I talking about? Ah, yes, advanced civilizations other than our own, both ancient and otherworldly. Evidence of lost civilizations exists all over the world, some buried in jungles, others submerged beneath our oceans. From the Bimini Road in the Bahamas and symmetrical stone structures found 650 meters below the surface of waters near Cuba to submerged structures near Japan and designs similar to those at Nazca found in the Gulf of California near Mexico, evidence of lost civilizations appear scattered around the globe. And not surprisingly, pyramid structures are among many of them. On land, ziggurats have been found covered by dense tropical growth or buried in desert sand. Ancient temples like Göbekli Tepe in Turkey share similar characteristics with many of these "lost cities." A vast subterranean labyrinth runs beneath the Pyramid at Giza, and yet we are not told of its history. And what about accounts of Agartha, a subterranean city said to exist deep beneath the Himalayas, a place described as being inhabited by guides that have instructed Dalai Llamas? From a more scientifically accepted end, in 2016, NASA's satellite imaging program "Ice Bridge" created a three-dimensional view of what was under the mile-thick sheet of ice covering Antarctica. It showed settlements, previously unknown landmasses, and structures, "some as big as the Eiffel Tower." Who built these structures, some dating back hundreds of thousands of years? And if you want to talk about sheer gross tonnage, there is no beating the Temple of Jupiter at Baalbek in Jerusalem, formerly known as Heliopolis. There, twenty-seven enormous, megalithic limestone blocks rest neatly on top of each other, each one weighing more than 800 tons, and which are so large that modern cranes would not be able to lift them. Other stones found at this ancient sight weigh as much as 1,200 tons, and in 2014, archaeologists found the mother of all blocks in a quarry there estimated to weigh 1,650 tons. We can't know for sure, of course, because there is no way for us to ever weigh the thing. Who was quarrying, moving, lifting, and placing such enormous stones with such precision seven thousand years ago? And more to the point, *why*?

Whenever these ancient ruins are discovered, people start making comparisons to the Lost Continent of Atlantis. Obviously, not all these structures can be Atlantis, but Atlantis is not the only "lost city" from antediluvian history. The so-called Lost Continents of Mu, Thule, and Lemuria come to mind. There were many places on earth that were lost to rising sea levels after the ice age ten thousand years ago. Others succumbed to landslides, volcanos, and other natural disasters. The point is, there are many of these lost cities and structures casting serious doubt on the officially accepted time line of history on this planet.

As Ford Prefect famously says in Douglas Adams's *The Hitchhiker's Guide to the Galaxy*, "Time is an illusion, lunchtime doubly so." This is true. All these civilizations still exist in their own times, just on different frequencies. And there are places, eddies, around the globe, where the frequencies tend to bleed together, the Veil becomes thin. Charles Berlitz, in his book *The Bermuda Triangle*, talks about the twelve "Vile Vortices" that exist equidistantly around our globe: five in the tropic of Cancer, five in the tropic of Capricorn, and one at either pole. The Bermuda Triangle is one, of course. These are particularly large eddies in the electromagnetic field. This Charles Berlitz is of the same Berlitz family that gave us the famous language schools, but he went in another direction. In his book on the Bermuda Triangle, he recounts the story of a priest who was invited out on a boat owned by members of his congregation to watch the Fourth of July fireworks over Miami from the ocean. As they sat out there in the Atlantic off the coast of Miami, the boat lost all power— lights, radio, everything. It was a very clear night, and the priest said he could see every star in the sky. As he was looking up at them, he noticed a black patch open up, blotting out some of the stars. Then he saw three lights drift across the sky and fly into the black patch, which then promptly closed up again, revealing the stars in their original places. And then all the power on their boat returned. He had seen some light craft passing out of our frequency and into the next via a portal in the Veil.

Sometimes these frequencies cross over like AM radio stations on a desert road at night. Some of you may not be old enough to recall this, but if you've ever been driving in a car at night, listening to the music on some all-night AM station, you might briefly hear an advertisement or announcement from another station bleed into the song. Usually, it bleeds out again, or you lose one station and find yourself tuned into another. It's like that. And it happens by accident sometimes. Keel's books are full of accounts from reliable people who report encounters with strange entities. Sometimes, rather than them slipping in over here, one of ours slips through to over there. There is the famous account of James Worson, a shoemaker from Leamington Spa, Warwickshire, England. In 1873, he took a drunken bet that he could run on foot from Leamington Spa to Coventry, a distance of approximately eighteen kilometers (eleven miles). As he ran, still drunk, he was followed by the two men he'd made the bet with, a linen draper and a photographer, their names are not important. As Worson ran, he suddenly lost his footing and stumbled forward with a terrible cry—and vanished before he hit the ground. He was never seen again. So let's look at the Veil.

CHAPTER 5

The Veil

The Veil is not a physical concept but a perceived one. Nothing outside our various corporeal frequencies is actually physical as we understand it, but there are different levels of perception. Depending on our spiritual development, we have access to one or more of these frequencies. This is going to be a hard chapter to write about.

The Veil is seen as physical to those of us that are incarnated, or corporeal, because everything to us, at least initially, is understood to be the same. It isn't until we start exploring the metaphysical that we come to realize that there are things that are not physical, and yet we still like to assign physical attributes to them to aid in our understanding or coping. I said this was going to be difficult for me to explain, but I also said I would be totally honest and open in sharing what I know and how I came to know it, and I told you this was going to get weird, so let me just jump right in. If you are troubled by it, you can always burn this book, but please don't burn me. Remember, I am only writing all this out because I wanted to try to help. Nonetheless, this is where this takes a more confessional turn. I mentioned earlier that I have been told these things. You probably asked, "Told by who?" Well, let's begin at the beginning again.

I was reincarnated into a very pleasant homelife. I had a loving family, and as far as I could tell, we wanted for nothing. Christmas at our home was always a time of plenty, and therefore, nothing got between me and the magical experience of that holiday. Also, looking back, I think our mother liked to make it extramagical by encouraging fantasies. If we saw a guy dressed as Santa walking into the neighbor's house, my mother told us we needed to go to bed so he wouldn't skip over our house. If we found a loose jingle bell on the floor (from a broken cat toy), she would tell us it must have fallen off an elf's hat—we were being watched! Christmas was always a happy and exciting time for my sister and me as children. We still felt that way right up until our early teens, waking up at 6:00 a.m. to raid our stockings and compare gifts. The rule in our house was that stockings were fair game upon waking, but no one touched the tree until we had breakfast together, and that didn't happen until our parents got out of bed. Long stories short, we were very fortunate.

My mother, as I said, was very loving. My big sister doted on me from the day they brought me home from the hospital. My father was a bit of a different story. He was distant. I learned later in life that he had been married before he met my mother. Nothing wrong with that. He had a rough life that came to an early end when he was forty-six and I was eleven. He died from his third heart attack. I learned more about him after his death. When he was alive, I feared him. He wasn't abusive that I can recall. He was just strict and racist. He yelled at my sister and me for playing with some Black children in our neighborhood. My mother told us he was wrong, but she also told us not to aggravate him.

My father had a brother, my uncle Jerry. The two of them had been abandoned when they were very young by their asshole of a father, a man we only knew as "The Colonel." I never met The Colonel, and I am glad I did not have that blight of a human being in my life, except by way of his influence on my father, which was bad enough. When their mother died, The Colonel had left my father and uncle with their maternal grandparents, poor dirt farmers in Bessemer, Alabama. As these poor folks could barely feed themselves, let alone two growing boys, they decided to turn the boys over to the state orphanage. My uncle overheard them planning this desperate act, and he and my father ran away to live as street children in New Orleans. I have no idea what that existence was like, and I can't imagine the horror of it. They subsisted somehow until they were old enough to lie about their ages and join the military. They both used my father's name to enlist as my uncle Jerry had by then earned a criminal record. Since they used the same name, they had to go into different branches, my uncle joining the Army and my father the Air Force. My father left the Air Force after his service because the military had integrated, and he did not like serving with Black men. He returned home and joined the Bessemer Police Force, where he was involved in the arrest of Martin Luther King Jr., not once but twice, for disturbing the peace.

To my father's credit, while he believed in segregation (a notion he shared with Malcolm X), he did not believe in violence against Blacks. He quit the Bessemer Police Force after witnessing his fellow officers beating the shit out of Dr. King while he was still in handcuffs. It was during this time that he married his first wife. I am unclear on the details. They had two children. I no longer speak to that side of the family. I met my half brother and half sister a few times throughout my childhood, but they always resented our family, and in particular, my mother. When they came up from Alabama for our father's funeral, my mother sat my sister and me down and said, "Be polite, be respectful, but do not get close to these people." Years later, when Facebook became a thing, we all connected there until my half sister, off her meds and high on attitude, sent me a message berating my sister and me and threatening my mother with murder. I disconnected from the lot of them then and there and have never looked back. But I digress.

My father reenlisted in the Air Force as an MP after he resigned from the Bessemer Ku Klux Kops, and it was during this time that he was sent for by the CIA, an agency evolved from the Office of Strategic Services. My father was summoned to a hotel room in Washington, DC, and was taken to meet a top dog in the growing agency. The top dog turned out to be the father he had not seen since being dumped at the doorstep of his maternal grandparents, The Colonel. The Colonel had worked for the OSS and was now recruiting for the CIA. All I know of this meeting is that my father essentially told his father that he would take the job with the CIA, but if The Colonel ever contacted him or his brother again, he would kill him. Soon after, my father was parachuting out of a plane and into Song Be, Vietnam, to run guns into Cambodia and discourage local farmers from giving weed to US soldiers. The CIA's base of operations in Song Be was a hospital, at which my mother happened to be working as a volunteer nurse. A few years later, along came I, born at the Holy Cross Hospital of Silver Spring, Maryland, barely two years after my mother had returned stateside to bring my sister into the world.

What does any of this have to do with the Veil? Well, nothing. I told you I would ramble. But it does serve to give you a bit of background that I will likely call upon in other parts of this book. I recall my earliest childhood memories so vividly that my sister often marvels, "How do you recall so much?" Well, Sissy (that was my baby name for her, "Sissy"), it takes practice. Sissy and I lived with my mom in a small basement apartment in a complex called Chelsea Woods in Maryland. There was another young couple, also government people, that helped my mom while my dad was still "in the field." We used to walk to the grocery store to go shopping, often stopping at a playground where my mother would push my sister and me on a merry-go-round. We moved when my father came home. I recall sitting on our floral-print couch with my mother and sister as movers boxed up our belongings and hauled them out to an orange semi-truck with a big "1" on the side... Route 1 Movers? I don't recall. (I just checked. My memory stands! It was indeed Route 1 Movers out of Virginia.) Anyway, we relocated to a townhouse in a place called Maid Stone Court, Virginia, just outside Langley. This was a neighborhood of spooks—all CIA and FBI people. My father had broken his leg in a training exercise, and he was home a lot during this period, so this is where my earliest memories of him come in. This is telling. Because of his late arrival, I viewed him as an outsider into our family unit that until then had consisted only of my mother, sister, and me. And he brought the angry voice of authority, so perhaps this is why we never really got close. My mother also took my sister and me to get our first dog at this time, a beagle mix we named Samantha, "Sam" for short. She was awesome. I recall we got her at a pet shop, where she had shared a little box with her brother. To this day, I am sorry we couldn't bring her brother home too. But Sam and my sister and I grew up happy.

Although I wasn't close to my father, and I did fear him in a way, I don't mean to give the impression that there was no love there. I do have many fond memories of him. Him putting a train track I had gotten for Christmas together. He didn't just do it, but he showed me how to do it. He'd tickle the hell out of me, and once, he gave me my first sip of beer as I sat on his lap during a football game. One of my all-time favorite movies is Mel Brooks's (really, Gene Wilder's) *Young Frankenstein* because a year before my father died, it was on network television, and he and I had watched it together. Actually, I watched it, and he watched me watch it, remarking with a big smile on his face, "I swear, I have never seen you laugh this hard!"

The Saturday morning when I awoke to my mother and my sister coming in and sitting on my bed to tell me that he had died was the first really hard day of my life. It was December 12, 1981. It was a Saturday. I cried for a solid two hours, sobbing uncontrollably. Then I settled down and watched *The Smurfs*. After that, I didn't cry again for the extent of the mourning period, not even at the funeral. I was more concerned for my mother. A very emotional woman, she cried whenever people on the street stopped to offer condolences. I wished they would just leave her alone, but that is the social norm. It is expected. She cried so much during this time, and I, soon becoming a teenaged asshole, made her cry even more. I will never be able to make up for that, and I will always be sorry. But that's for me to work out. Finally, this brings us to the Veil.

After my father died, I had a very strange dream. In the dream, I awoke in my room and heard the TV on in the living room. I used to fall asleep listening to the TV as my parents stayed up to watch "late shows" after my sister and I were in bed. I still like to fall asleep to the sound of a TV in the other room. However, I knew it was too late for anyone to be up watching TV. So I walked out to the living room, and there was my father, sitting in his chair. Sam was at his feet, all wiggles, the loyal dog excited to see the Big Man. I knew he shouldn't be there. I knew he was dead. He turned and looked at me, smiled, and stood up. "Mattamus!" he said. That was his nickname for me: Mattamus Q. Fattamus because I had been a chubby baby, which had delighted him. He showed me a small wound on his arm, on the inside of his elbow. "Look! That's where they stuck the IV!" he said. I turned and ran down the hallway and into my mother's room. I woke her up and said, "Dad's here!" She followed me out into the living room, and by now, my sister had been awakened by the commotion, and she came out too. We all saw my father, standing over the dog, who was still all wiggly and happy to see him, showing her the scar on his arm. My mother grabbed my sister and me and pulled us into the hallway bathroom. I still recall clearly seeing the blue-and-white tiles of the bathroom floor. My mother was crying, and I asked, "Can we move?" I didn't want to live in a haunted house. She nodded, and that was all I recall of the dream. Less than a year later, in the "real" world, we moved to a house just a block away.

It was while we lived in that new house that I started communicating with another consciousness. It was then that I learned about the Veil. During that period of my life, I began to isolate myself. I didn't spend much time with my friends. They had all begun to drift away from me, probably because I had started to become "weird." I will tell you now that this was a turning point in my life. It could have gone very dark if it hadn't been for this new line of communication with a higher consciousness. I was told to keep everything I learned secret/sacred. I use the "/" there because I realized that when I "spoke" to this consciousness, the word used sounded like both and carried the same meaning. They became synonymous in my thinking. Looking back on my life before this, I started to recall moments of peculiarity, things that I hadn't noticed at the time, things that I had chalked up to the childhood mindset. When we see things that don't fit into, or outright contradict, our base understanding of reality, we tend to let them slip past the conscious mind and right into the subconscious, where they become the stuff of dreams. This is called "negative hallucination"—not seeing something that is there. I'll talk more about negative hallucination when discussing seeing otherworldly entities, so watch for it.

While my father was still alive, and we lived in the other house, my family had been sitting on our back deck one June evening. I was around eight or nine years old. My parents sat on deck chairs, and my sister and I had pulled our bean bag chairs that we had gotten for

Christmas the previous year out and were nestled in those. It was a beautiful night, the sky was clear, and as I'd mentioned before, out on the edge of town where we lived, you could see the full glory of the Milky Way above. Real Pennsylvania country skies. And my mother said, "Now what do you suppose that is?" "That" was a reddish-or-ange orb, about the size of a basketball from where we sat, zigzagging across the clear country sky. It looked small due to distance, and it appeared to be over nearby Pickle Hill that dominated the landscape behind our house. We watched it move in a seemingly random pattern, and my father—former Air Force and CIA, remember—was dumbfounded. "What the hell moves like that?" I recall it because I had never seen my father so baffled. And honestly, I don't recall how the evening ended. I just have that memory. Years later, when we lived in the new house, my neighborhood friend and I would still play in that field behind our houses. One night, we saw a large white oval-shaped object cruise silently over our heads. I jumped up and started waving at it, and my friend grabbed me and pushed me to the ground. "Stop!" he said. "You don't want them to see us!" I don't want *who* to see us? And why? The egg-shaped object turned and silently disappeared over Pickle Hill.

There was definitely something about this little patch of North-Central Pennsylvania. And as I grew up, around the age of thirteen, I began to talk to…it. And as I said, I was in a dark time of my life then, and if it weren't for this extra education, I might have been a very different person in a very ugly way. And I use the word "education" because that is exactly what it was. I wasn't getting it from school at the time. We lived in a very small town (we only had one traffic light until they built the Walmart in 1994), and my high school experience reflected that in every way, which isn't as pleasant as it may sound. It wasn't so much an education in knowledge but in survival as I was one that drew the attention of bullies all too often. Each morning, I would fight my poor mother tooth and nail not to go to school, and she was a newly single mom working as a full-time nurse to make sure my sister and I still had full, happy Christmases. And I was just an asshole, and I will never, ever be able to be sorry enough. The school and others probably blamed her for my frequent absences, writing good-natured notes for me every time I finally had to return to school: "Please excuse Matthew from school. He had a bad case of schoolitis!" Haha. That poor woman. I must have been such an exhausting, stressful embarrassment to her. It was all my fault. She deserves a high seat in "heaven" (the highest frequencies) for all she did for and put up with from me.

I would spend my evenings in our backyard, looking up at those amazing stars. I recalled my sigil through a physical gesture I had taught myself, and all this information came flooding back into my conscious mind. Keep in mind, sigils do not require a correlating physical gesture, but I had apparently assigned one to mine due to a past life in which I had been deaf. To this day, I have a strong affinity for the beauty of sign language. Of all the languages I could learn, I was drawn to that one early on. Thing is, what good does a physical gesture do for a sigil? When you need it the most, you have no physical form with which to make the gesture. Well, not always. Many people retain a sort of psychic projection of their physical form purely out of habit. They've been in the physical form so long their minds identify with it. Most people tend to mistake their bodies for themselves, and this is how it usually transfers over to the ethereal. If you've been through the life-death-life cycle enough times, you are more comfortable with being a consciousness without the need of any defined form. My first realization of this, after what feels like it may have been my third recalled transformation, was the lack of a face. You sense so much through the holes in your physical face, the air drawing in through the mouth and nostrils, for example, you notice that missing almost immediately. At first, you're not even aware of what feels so different, but you soon realize.

What was I saying? Ah, yes, when I consciously recalled my sigil, all these thoughts and memories came flooding back with it, like uncorking a shaken champagne bottle. I felt a connection and ideas that were not my own began to connect with those that I was recalling, filling in missing data (the barrel-of-monkeys method). I recalled the gesture as a greeting so that when I met these entities, I could signal that I was with them. I learned that death is a doorway, a simple transition, and that I have nothing to fear. Don't worry, this isn't going to become one of those angsty teen novels about struggles with suicidal thoughts. On the contrary, these evening meditations gave me a love for life, a profound respect for life, and a love for all living things. It didn't happen all at once, of course. It was a gradual process, like all worthwhile lessons. Now come some hard confessions, but I have to share them here to help express just how pivotal this was for me. So here we go.

I dropped out of high school around this time. My mother gave in. She just couldn't fight me anymore, and she had faith in me because we had started having long evening talks when she got home from work. She even recorded them so that she could play them for my therapist. I agreed to this because I had come to understand her struggle to defend me, and I wanted to help. These conversations would not have been possible if it hadn't been for my other contact. She was so scared for me, but I was able to assuage her fears and explain what I had planned for my life. She accepted it. In fact, she was relieved by it. If it hadn't been for her being so understanding and open-minded, I never could have continued. And I know she took the brunt of judgment from our little town—the kind of place where everyone knew each other's business and were happy to share their opinions behind your backs. My mom stood by me. And it is good that she did because if it hadn't been for my secret education and her support, I very well could have become a serial killer.

This may be a tad hyperbolic, but at the age of fifteen, I fit the profile of the FBI's signs of the early development of a serial killer criteria as described in Robert Ressler's book *Whoever Fights Monsters* a wee bit too closely. Ressler is the guy who basically created the FBI's infamous Behavioral Sciences Unit, as portrayed in the Netflix series *Mindhunter*, which is based on his book. I never went so dark as to torture or kill animals, but everything else? As Midwesterners might say, "You betcha!" Fortunately, I came away from it as a relatively decent human being, a caring, loving entity with golden respect for all life. Had that higher consciousness not tapped me, I could have gone down a very different path. It was also during this time that I developed a severe sort of obsessive-compulsive disorder that still nags me to this day. When it first developed in me, around the age of thirteen, it was triggered by my school. When I got home, I felt like I was covered in dust and needed to take a cold shower. Even today, when I am stressed with this OCD, I need cold water to "wash it away." After I dropped out of school, it became centered on interactions with my family. I often think that had it not been for this OCD driving me away from my family, I very easily could have become the sort of recluse that lives in his mother's basement. And I don't mean to shame those that do live in their parents' basement. The world can be a hard and intimidating place and not everyone is ready for it or is in an environment conducive to confronting it. I guess I should be thankful for my own insecurities forcing me out into the world, but it still breaks my heart to think of all the lost time I should have spent with my family. I am not sure where this OCD really stems from, but it has to do with my physical appearance. I will just chalk it up to an inexcusable amount of vanity. I have tried on several occasions to override it, rise above it, and although I have managed to make it manageable without the need of medication, I always fail at irradicating it completely. I assume it is some unknown holdover from a past life memory.

Changing the subject to make myself feel better...

I was on a flight just about a year ago from South Korea to visit a friend in New Zealand. It was wintertime in the northern hemisphere and summer in the southern, and somewhere along the way, we hit some major turbulence. I was sitting at the end of the middle section of seats in the economy (or cattle) class, and there was a woman sitting on the other end of my row. There was no one between us, and man, isn't that nice when you're flying coach? So up until we hit turbulence, we were both very comfortable. Once the turbulence went from "Oh, this is nothing scary, just a part of flying" to "Oh shit, planes are made of tinfoil!" the woman beside me started to put off an energy of extreme uneasiness. It wasn't just her. Several people around the cabin had begun to exchange nervous glances and uneasy laughter when the cabin crew took their seats and strapped in. Then came a big hit, and the entire plane seemed to drop several feet so fast it felt like a roller coaster in our stomachs. There were audible gasps, and I glanced over at the woman, and she glanced back, eyes white all around as she clutched her armrest. I smiled reassuringly at her and shrugged: "It's fine." When we were past the turbulence and normality had been restored, she asked me, "How can you look so calm when the plane is shaking like that?" I chuckled a bit and said, "Ah, what's the worst that could happen?" She laughed nervously and said, "I don't even want to think about it." I replied, "It's nothing we haven't all done before." She gave me a look that suggested I had said something odd. We struck up a conversation. She was a Kiwi returning home to visit family in Auckland from her home in Amsterdam. She asked if I was American, and I said that I was. Is it just me, or does anyone else feel a tinge of insult when someone asks if you're an American? What gave me away—was I being loud or offensive? Did I say something ignorant? Are you saying I'm obese? Americans don't have the best global reputation these days. After we had landed and were engaged in the endless process of taxiing to a gate, she asked, "What did you mean when you said it's nothing we haven't done before?" I replied, "Well, if the plane were to go down and everyone thinks they're going to die, it's good to remember that dying is nothing new or scary. When you actually face it, it's comfortingly familiar." She asked, "How would you know that?" "Because I remember it. I've reincarnated. And so have you, and probably so has everyone else on this plane." She stared at me for a moment and then said, "You Americans are strange." I laughed, and she glanced back at me, and she laughed too. We didn't speak again until we had collected our belongings from the overhead bins and began filing out of the aircraft. She just smiled at me and said, "It was lovely to meet you. Enjoy New Zealand!"

I don't know what she actually thought of our conversation or what she may have said about me later to her friends that came to meet her at the airport, but for me, that was a good experience. I hope she started to think about it beyond "Americans are strange." Everyone is strange in some way or another, it seems. If they're not, then they're boring. They need to rack up some experiences.

So that is death: nothing new. As I have said before, death is just moving to a state of being outside the corporeal, outside of time, where our consciousness or soul encounters everything in the real world, all at once and unfiltered. It can be overwhelming. This is why you should have a sigil to focus on to carry you through it to another incarnation in case you are not quite integrated enough to handle it all. Not everyone incarnates on the same frequency, however. There are souls that incarnate on corporeal levels totally removed from the one we are currently in. These other frequencies are separated by the Veil. I am no physicist, so the best way I can describe it is as an electromagnetic frequency or a quantum vibrational frequency. When I was just starting down this esoteric path, I often wondered, "If these other worlds exist all around us, how are we not bumping into these other entities all the time?" The short answer is, we sometimes do. But it is so rare an occasion because there are few places where frequencies cross accidentally, and humans and other incarnate creatures tend to avoid them.

Again, I'm not a physicist, but as it was explained to me, corporeal matter contains a lot of empty space. Although it appears solid to us, the empty space between atoms and the subatomic is actually quite vast. To put it mathematically, it is like the distance between 1 and 2. One might think there is no distance between these two digits when, in fact, there is an infinity of space between these two numbers. Somewhere in there, you have the numbers 1.0000000000000001 and 1.00000017 and $1.000000000800000000000000001$ and so on, a numeric infinity between 1 and 2. Everything vibrates to a certain frequency. In this way, other worlds can exist all around us, "in our midst" as the Christ teaches, passing right through us unseen and undetected all the time. As H. P. Lovecraft is alleged to have written in the *Necronomicon*, a book attributed publicly to someone known as Abdul Al-Hazred, the "Mad Arab," (whom most literary scholars believe to have really been that mad racist Lovecraft), they walk "not in the spaces we know, but between them." Think of the propellor on a Sopwith Camel, the World War I-era plane. The machine gun on this plane was positioned directly behind the propellor, but the firing mechanism was timed so precisely that the bullets would pass cleanly between the spinning blades of the propellor. The propellor, when spinning, looks to the eye like a near-solid disc, and yet solid projectiles can pass safely through it without touching it. It's not perfect, but that's the analogy I was given at the time. Similarly, solid objects on another frequency can pass right through us. Like radio waves, what you perceive depends on the frequency you are tuned into.

Is it possible to tune into these other frequencies and see these other worlds? Absolutely. It does take a lot of meditative practice, however. I have read accounts of Buddhist monks who have been able to change their physical vibrational frequency and walk through solid objects. Others can astral project their consciousness out of their physical bodies to cross into these other realms. It is not for the uninitiated, and it can be dangerous, so it is not something that is easily attainable. We can't just have everybody popping in and out of different frequencies willy-nilly, after all. Most commonly, it is a sort of broadcast frequency—a cross-frequency conversation—that takes place rather than a full manifestation or projection into these other worlds. It's the difference between speaking to someone through a closed door rather than just walking right through the closed door and shaking their hand. This is not to say that the latter never happens. Our histories are full of accounts of this very phenomenon. As mentioned earlier, check out the works of Fortean researcher John Keel or just read the holy books of our world from the Bible to the Bhagavad Gita (Mahabharata, I just like the alliteration).

Entire civilizations have passed into higher or lower frequencies, risen to better ones or dropped down to darker ones. The Lost Civilization of Atlantis, for example, to us is only a legend and some circular markings left on the dry soil of North Africa. It still exists, but not where we can yet interact with it. When the Earth tilted in what we call the antediluvian epoch, the Earth's electromagnetic fields shifted suddenly, and the result was the transition of what we call Atlantis. The perfect hexagon on the north pole of Saturn, from our perspective, is just that a perfect two-dimensional geometric shape although perfectly geometrical shapes do not happen by accident. On another frequency, it is a cube. What its purpose is, I have no idea. I asked and was told it is some sort of a forge for conscious energies that exist on the lower frequencies, a "hell" in which consciousness is shredded in a terrible maelstrom. This is why Saturn has always been aligned with the concept of Satan in our ancient occult. Interestingly, the symbol of Saturn is the Star of David, which is a hexagram (a six-pointed star with a hexagon at its center). Modern organized religion has found it convenient to lump all nondogmatic entities under one umbrella, one character. God is God, angels are angels, and the devil is everything else. As I said before, there are billions of entities, and they run the gamut from truly evil to truly good and everything in between, as all individuals do. Many civilizations lost to this world still exist in other time lines and frequencies—they have just shifted in their wavelengths. This is true of a civilization that existed on the island of Hy Brasil in the Atlantic Ocean west of Ireland. Their advanced civilization is still there, imperceivable to us in our time and frequency. The island itself is "submerged" to us but legend says that at certain times, when the conditions are right, people have reported seeing the island materialize. It reminds one of Brigadoon. Yet although this civilization is "lost" to us, they maintain contact and continue to observe our progress. If you have ever read about the Rendlesham Forest UFO incident, then you will be somewhat familiar with Hy Brasil.

To summarize, the Rendlesham Forest UFO incident recounts ultraterrestrial contact made by US Air Force personnel stationed at RAF Woodbridge in the United Kingdom. The Royal Air Force had leased the base to the Americans during the Cold War until 1993. The account goes that USAF officers had witnessed white, orange, and blue-green lights in the forest over the twenty-sixth and twenty-eighth of December 1980. Going out to investigate, USAF officers described finding a landed craft, triangular in shape, and made of opaque black glass that was marked all around with "strange hieroglyphics." There was an audio recording made during the incident by the officers on the ground that was released to the public. They described the craft as resting on three legs, and the next day, three indentations in the ground in a triangular formation were found, and high radiation levels were detected, suggesting the craft was experiencing technical issues. One of the USAF officers touched the object and claimed that he received a mental image of 1s and 0s—binary code that was recorded in his memory. He wrote the binary message in his notebook, and it was later decoded. The message, although broken, mentions "exploration of humanity," "continuous for planetary advance," and "Fourth coordinate," and then lists a short series of earth-based coordinates in our frequency: 16.763177N 89.11768W (Caracci, Belize), 34.800272N 111.843567W (Sedona, Arizona), 29.977836N 31.131649E (Great Pyramid, Giza, Egypt), 14.701505S 75.167043W (Nazca Lines, Peru), 36.256845N 117.100632E (Tai Shan Qu, China), and 37.110195N 25.372281E (Portara at Temple of Apollo, Naxos, Greece). The list is bookended with the same coordinates, 52.0942532N 13.131269W—Hy Brasil. The message also contains the phrase "Eyes of your eyes" and "Origin year 8100." If one is to go by what we know about some of these coordinates, specifically, Nazca, Peru, and the Great Pyramid at Giza, then this would seem to support my information that these locations are often used as markers for travelers from beyond our world.

Just as all frequencies, Veil frequencies range from lower to higher. The lower frequencies are more attuned to the concept of hell while the higher frequencies are more attuned to the concept of heaven. Think of it as the sea—as pressure and atmosphere change with depth, atmospheric changes may occur between frequency realms, and the farther down you go, the less light there is and the uglier the creatures become. Have you ever seen an angler fish or a goblin shark? However, the higher up you go, the more light there is, the bluer the waters, and the more beautiful the inhabitants. Hopefully, you've seen dolphins. The energy, or frequency, you tune in to pulls you closer to these frequencies: fear and hate, the lower you go. Love and joy, the higher. This is why I said earlier that you should go into death with a profound feeling of love and joy.

Our world is endangered by the influence of the lower frequencies and the consciousnesses that reside there. Our reality, our frequency, is being pulled into these lower frequencies. Earlier, I spoke of collective consciousness, and the Princeton EGG experiment, the Global Consciousness Project. As our global consciousness becomes more connected and synchronized via mass media, we are being fed an emotional diet that tends to consist mostly of the negative: fear and hate. And this is not accidental. Before I talk about this, however, I would like to share another story. This story will get its own chapter because this chapter has already gone on too long.

CHAPTER 6

Fifth-Column Franklin

This is an account copied directly from one of my personal journals. It will repeat some points I have already mentioned, but this will happen a lot throughout this book. As I have warned before, I am scatterbrained by trying to share this information and don't feel I have the time to try to edit it without doing irreparable damage to it. Keep in mind, it is not all that uncommon to encounter entities from beyond the Veil. In fact, you may well have met one or more in your time in this life and not been aware of it—or perhaps you are aware of it and have a story to tell. I would love to hear it. From the odd tales handed down over centuries, like the green bean-eating children of Woolpit, to modern accounts of the Men in Black, these entities have walked among us since the dawn of our history. In fact, Men in Black are spoken of long before the UFO craze of the twentieth century. And keep in mind, although they are charged with keeping our progress orderly by restricting certain information, these "MiB" as we call them are not "bad" entities. They have never actually harmed anyone. Well, except for one account, but I believe that to be a case of mistaken identity. And they are not at all like they are portrayed in the movies of the same name. Here is my account of a conversation I had with a friend of mine that I have had the pleasure of hanging out with on two separate occasions.

Fifth-Column Franklin

I just had the awkward experience of having a friend come out to me. And he's not gay or pansexual or anything like that (not that there's anything wrong with that). Actually, he came out to me as an alien. And not just from another country but from an entirely different civilization. How am I supposed to respond to that?

Obviously, I cannot use my friend's real name, so I am calling him "Franklin" for the sake of this article. My reasoning for this name choice is twofold: (1) it offers a nice alliteration to the term "fifth column," which will come into play in a big way later in the article, and (2) a song I like called "Franklin's Tower."

So what does all this mean? I really have no idea. All I can do is relate to you the events leading up to this peculiar disclosure. You see, I teach. Sort of. It's hard to explain. Actually, it's very easy to explain, but it's very boring, so I will just say it's hard to explain and move on. Nonetheless, one of my favorite points to bring up in a lecture each semester is how wording is everything, and synonyms can be very powerful tools of misdirection. I begin by showing my students a short YouTube video about the "Government Cover-Up of Alien Life"—whichever one is recent and well-made, but any of the thousands that exist will do. And then I open the floor to comments. After a nice discussion has been started over the existence of extraterrestrials and whether or not they have visited earth—and interestingly, this topic always sparks a lively discussion among students, who by nature refuse to speak at all, and each year, I notice more students fall on the side of true believers—I make them a bet. The bet goes like this: I will bet you that I can prove, beyond any doubt, that UFOs are real and that aliens walk on earth among us." They always stare at me for a second and then ask for points of clarification, to which I respond, "No clarification needed, that's it. I can prove to you, right now, that UFOs are very real, and that there are aliens walking on this earth—right here in this very community, in fact. No trickery."

Usually, they take the bet. Sadly, the university has rules against gambling and against professors taking money from students, so I have to make it a bet for something like extra homework, which I hate as much as they do. After they have taken the bet, I remind them that "UFO" does not mean "alien spaceship." It is simply an acronym for Unidentified Flying Object, and the skies are full of those, whether they be drones, unmarked aircraft, Chinese lanterns, or alien spaceships. As for "aliens walk among us," I simply show them my Alien Registration Card, which states that I am a registered visitor from another country. I then remind them that the word "alien" does not have to mean "space alien" and that anyone with citizenship from one country who lives in another country is by definition an alien.

This explanation is usually met with groans from the students. But I digress. This past semester, I had a friend visiting. This friend is, of course, the aforementioned Franklin, and he sat in on my lecture so that we could go out drinking right after. And we did. At first, right after leaving campus, he seemed very quiet and distracted, which is unusual for Franklin. He's usually quite chatty. Three short hours later, we were in a nice local pub and feeling a bit intoxicated. Franklin had begun to be his usual talkative self, and he finally got around to complimenting me on my lecture and said he enjoyed the bet about the aliens walking among us. Of course, he followed this up with, "What would you say if I told you that I was an alien from a different world?" I replied, "Is your name Ford Prefect?" referencing the book *The Hitchhiker's Guide to the Galaxy* by Douglas Adams, a liking of which I recalled had been a commonality that had cemented our early friendship.

Well, you can imagine how the rest of this conversation went. I won't bore you with the details, mainly because I cannot recall most of them. The more I made fun of him for trying to trick me, the more he seemed to enjoy feeding me bits of information that would result in a raised eyebrow or a rare moment of stunned silence as I tried to think of another wisecrack to break the awkward silence. He mentioned being part of a group of observers from "beyond the Veil" (as he put it) between our two civilizations. He assured me that he was human, from a purely genetic perspective, but that his biological form had been enhanced with nanotechnology, which prevented him from getting sick, gave him an eidetic and photographic memory (a distinction which he had to explain to me), and could, if he so chose, halt his aging process at any time. It was at this point that I found myself thinking about how I had known him for nearly fifteen years and yet he didn't seem to have aged all that much, certainly not as much as I had.

I recall him asking the bartender for a deck of cards, which all good bartenders keep behind the bar for the occasional card trick that drunks like to try to show off every once in a while. Franklin had me shuffle the cards and then start laying them down, faceup, one on top of another. I went through half the deck, and he stopped me by saying, "Okay, that's enough." He then told me to pick up the cards and fan them out, backs to him, and follow along as he named each and every card in the correct order without being able to see them. That was impressive to me, but then I was pretty drunk at the time. Thinking back on it now in the sober light of day, it's still pretty damned impressive.

Franklin also speaks my language (English, obviously), his native language (French, for some reason), and the language of the country we were drinking in, all fluently. I have never asked him how many languages he can speak, but he never seems to have any trouble with any languages he encounters.

We did some shots. We invited the bartender to join us when we handed the playing cards back over to her. After the shots and some mild flirting, she ran far away and left us to continue our chat. I felt I had run out of jokes at this point as that card trick had left me wondering. After all, I am one of those true believers. I do honestly believe—no, there is no belief needed at this point. I am *aware* that there is at least one extraterrestrial presence involved here on earth, and I was aware of this before Franklin decided to come out to me. I asked him, "Why now, Franklin? And why are you telling *me*?" He replied that I had an open mind and he had enjoyed how I addressed the topic with my students and that we had discussed the issue before, I just couldn't recall our previous conversation.

We ended up back in his hotel room because I like drinking in hotels, and he wanted to show me something that he could not show me in public, not even if he whipped it out in the privacy of the men's room because someone could walk in on us and leave him with a lot of explaining to do. Sounds shameful, doesn't it? Well, it's going to be a disappointing story for you if you are hoping this will take that sort of a turn. What he had to show me was a small device, handheld, and looked like a dildo, I shit you not. And still, I tell you this is *not* that sort of story. This device emitted sound waves somewhere in the 8 MHz to 20 MHz range (if I recall correctly. Unlike Franklin, I am not good with numbers). Whatever range it is, it is not audible to humans or animals, he said. I certainly couldn't hear it. At the lower range, I thought I could almost hear a faint whirring sound, but what do I know? I was drunk. And I didn't have a cat with me to test the animal claim.

We went into the bathroom, and Franklin turned on the shower. He held the device under the water, and the water moved around the object. It didn't get hit with a single drop. Fully clothed, he got into the shower with the device, and the water arched over him like he was holding an invisible umbrella, which, he said, he was. He let me try it. I stood there in the shower, a bottle of beer in one hand and Franklin's magic dildo in the other, howling that that was the most amazing thing I had ever seen. He was grinning. "See?" he said. "It's a simple technology, and yet your side hasn't come up with it yet! You've had your cumbersome umbrellas for, what, over four

thousand years now, and still no new developments? We're going to give you another seven to
ten years, and if no one has developed it by then,
then we're going to seed it out to you." He paused
and then added, "Probably."

I asked him what he meant by "probably"
despite all the other questions that were clamber-
ing at the forefront of my skull. He said sometimes he hears they will "seed" something, and
they never do. Sometimes, things just pop up
in our open market, like Wi-Fi and such. I told
him Wi-Fi was invented by the military, and he
said, "No, actually, one of us seeded it back in the
1960s. Eva Kiesler, but she was known to your
people as Hedy Lamarr, an actress." I thought he
had made a *Blazing Saddles* joke, so I laughingly
corrected him, "Hedley!" He looked confused
for a second then recalled that line from the clas-
sic Gene Wilder/Mel Brooks movie and smiled.
"See?" he said. "That's why I'm telling you all
this. You're intelligent, laid-back, and you have
the sense of humor to roll with it." I was touched.
I really do think that is the nicest compliment
anyone has ever paid me. I was so delighted by
the comment that I forgot about the odd Hedy
Lamarr reference. (I checked it out later and
damned if he wasn't right.) Instead, I stepped out
of the shower, still bone-dry, and asked him what
other tricks he had in the bag. He adjusted something on the magic dildo and inserted it into the
wall—*into the wall.* The thing just slipped right
into the plaster, right through it, leaving only a
slightly blurry ring around the point of penetra-
tion. It literally went through a solid wall without
breaking it. It didn't even do so much as tearing the wallpaper. He moved it around and then

pulled it back out and shut it off. I was dumb-struck. He walked out of the bathroom, leaving me there, running my hands over the still-intact solid wall like one of the apes poking the mono-lith at the beginning of *2001: A Space Odyssey.*

After I had found my way out of the bath-room, he tossed the object to me, but I was afraid to even touch it, so it landed on the car-peted floor with a light thump. He chuckled at my apparent primitive fear of the inexplicable and explained that it used microsound waves to change the vibration frequency of atoms so that seemingly "solid" objects could pass right through one another. The device he had shown me was a multipurpose tool. Rain-diverting devices were usually just tiny soundwave emitters sewn into clothing, such as hats.

He said frequencies could carry over (syn-chronize) from one solid object to another and allow living beings to pass through solid walls. He also said that sound waves could lift heavy objects by changing the vibrational frequencies of the atmosphere around them. I asked when they were going to seed that technology to our civilization, and he said they weren't. Keeping us out of the rain was one thing, but giving us the ability to walk through walls could easily be abused by certain factions within our society. He said they thought of us as children, and they had to be the strict parents who decided when we were responsible enough to get the latest toys.

At this point, what with the booze and the magic tricks, my head was spinning. We sat down at the awkward little hotel table and opened a couple of more beers as he laid out the history of his people. I am writing from memory, so consider the following to be the abridged version:

Human beings are a hybrid species created thousands of years ago as a labor force by an advanced species from another planet. Most people are already familiar with this scenario, so I won't spend much time on it. The written record that became the book of Genesis offers a very broad description of how these "Great Ones" created our species by genetically modifying Australopithecus with their own DNA. For a while, they lived quite comfortably on our backs and treated us like slaves. There was a social hierarchy, and the early humans that found favor with the Great Ones ("gods") were treated as beloved pets while the rest were used as a disposable labor force. Indeed, the "God" of the Old Testament was not a very nice entity. However, there were "animal lovers" within that alien society who took it upon themselves to try to educate the new labor force and teach them how they could become more than just pack mules.

This caused some conflict among their race, and it resulted in a war that decimated our earlier civilizations. This war caught the attention of *ultraterrestrials* or pandimensional beings that exist here on earth. Franklin explained that dimensions aren't so much "other universes" as they are other worlds that exist on another frequency, different from our own. These pandimensionals did not like what the Great Ones had been doing. Creating a hybrid sentient species was very much frowned upon, and not only by the pandimensionals but by the ruling class of the home planet of our creators. A truce was struck, and it was decided that humans would be quarantined, and a sort of noninvolvement treaty was created for all the advanced civilizations. Rather than wipe us out entirely, they would cull the herd and introduce a system of government with a human leadership that would take over after a sort of educational period during which we were ruled from afar by a joint interim government of the extra- and ultraterrestrials. As they withdrew and were less visible to new generations of humans, they slipped into legend as their human liaisons assumed the duties of direct rule over the lower classes. These human leaders became kings. These lineages still survive today.

Not all the early humans were left to their own devices, however. Some who had found favor were adopted by some of the ET and UT entities and were taken to travel with them (read "taken up to walk with God"). These "chosen few" were allowed to coexist in an advanced civilization that was created with more of a hands-on approach within another dimension here on earth: the "Gatherings beyond the Veil" as Franklin called it. They still act as a sort of liaison civilization between ours and the world of what we would have called "gods." As early human civilization developed, conflicts arose in support of various gods like drunks screaming about football teams, so it was decided to provide a sort of "world religion" that offered only one god. It helped a little, but...well, look at us today. We generally accept the idea of one God, so now we kill each other over how best to worship it. Still, the laws of noninterference have only grown stronger among the UTs (the ETs are still here, but there are many different races—four that Franklin knows of although he suspects there may be more that have just gone unrecognized up to now). They seem to feel it is best for everyone if they keep their distance, considering what a primitive and volatile civilization ours is. Still, direction is handed down via the gatherings (cities) beyond the Veil (i.e., Franklin's people since they can easily blend in with our society). Of course, over the millennia, even that leadership has fractured into vying factions, each with their own philosophy on how best to deal with the "human problem." These philosophies range from direct rule to outright extermination and everything in between.

Franklin is part of what he calls a "fifth column," a group of spiritually motivated UTs that live among us as on-site observers and sometime-guides. They feel it is in the best interest of all if they let humans evolve generally unmolested, offering guidance and technology where it is needed although the technology is very rarely offered, and when it is, it is only after long and thorough debate. The magic dildo he showed me is more along the lines of "next-step development," meaning it is not too far removed from technologies that we are already familiar with, and so it doesn't seem too shocking—that is, not shocking enough to knock us off our intended path of development. He showed me a sort of manual that they use to determine what information to share. Not all the information is factual—some of it is used intentionally to deceive in order to manipulate our leaders into taking a particular course of action that they might otherwise have avoided. It seemed very complicated, like a chess game in which one side is able to plan eight moves in advance, if not already have the entire game figured out and won before the board is even set up.

For now, I will summarize: New technologies are introduced to our civilization only if we cannot pick up on the "inspiration" that is often provided through the more imaginative, intelligent, and open members of our society (open, that is, to subconscious grooming through dreams, extreme-low-frequency messages, and other vague communications). Minds like that of Nikola Tesla are more susceptible to these subtler communiqués, and these (un)fortunate people are often remembered by us as geniuses and visionaries. New technologies can only be introduced if there can be a logical tracing from our current tech to the next-level stuff. Very rarely does something truly earth-shattering get through, and quite often, these breakthroughs are accidental. There was quite a panic on both sides of the Veil when they detonated that first atomic bomb at Alamogordo. Apparently, atomic bombs have a negative impact not just on our side of the vibrational barriers. If you die in a nuclear blast, in that you get vaporized, there is no reincarnation. Your soul is vaporized along with your physical form. This is why ETs and UTs have taken such a dire interest in our nuclear weapons. This caused a rush of activity resulting in further carelessness, and we ended up getting the wreckage from Roswell. Guess what was housed at the Roswell Army Airfield at the time? The US's only stockpile of nuclear weapons.

Franklin talked, and I listened for the entire night, and before I knew it, it was getting light outside. Franklin said there was so much more to tell, but he had covered the basics. He ended on a warning, a reminder that he is not the only faction at work at manipulating our civilization. There is a more menacing factor that has taken a much more direct approach by infiltrating the top echelons of world governments, most notably in the United States. These people have one goal: to either enslave us or to get humanity to destroy itself. The extinction of our species will raise a lot of eyebrows if not done correctly, as it is a direct violation of the previously mentioned treaty of governance. If these entities directly attack and annihilate us, they could very well face the same retaliation by the other members of the treaty. However, they believe that we represent a clear and present danger to all worlds and therefore should be wiped out of existence. And since direct interference on that scale would certainly draw the ire of every sentient civilization currently observing this mess, they have opted for slow suicide. They give us just enough rope to hang ourselves, turning us against one another, encouraging us to kill ourselves. They don't murder us outright. Instead, they give us the gun and convince us to shoot ourselves in the head. Think of Hannibal Lecter whispering to Multiple Miggs in his cell at the lunatic asylum in *Silence of the Lambs*. Lecter, a hyperintelligent entity, was offended by the crass abomination in the cell next door, so he directs him into self-destruction.

These entities will see us destroy ourselves, if not with open warfare, then with our own waste. They feed the greed that is inherent in our species, creating a ruling elite class that is centered in the reptilian part of the human brain, the part of the brain that focuses on greed, power, and self-preservation. They don't care about you or me—in fact, they want us all dead. And they are making great strides each and every day to ensure that we will not survive another hundred years. Just look at the laws currently being passed or lifted by the US Congress. If they don't scream self-destruction, nothing does. Once we have destroyed ourselves to the point of nonredemption, they will be given the all-clear to finish us off. Mitch McConnell and his ilk are big tools in the development of this plan. Donald Trump was a bull in the china shop. Again, I don't wish to politicize this because both sides of the political puppet show have been infiltrated and would have us marching to the same killing floor. It's not really a question of politics but one of wealth and access. The funny thing is, these greedy "elites" believe that when it's all said and done, they will be spared and allowed into the "promised land" beyond the Veil. Nope. According to Franklin, they, too, will be left to die here, probably facing a more horrifying death than the rest of us just for being greedy assholes. Either way, at this rate, we should be ripe for extermination within the next hundred years.

Franklin's group is aware of this plot and is trying to drum up support to counteract it, but so far, it is hard to get anyone on his side of the curtain to give a damn about us. They are also a developing civilization, albeit a far more advanced one, both spiritually and technologically, and they have their own problems on their own level with which to contend. As for the alien races from this dimension, they seem to be content in watching us as though we were entertainment. Indeed, the moon itself is apparently a huge observation platform upon which we lower humans were never meant to tread.

From time to time, they do make contact, but their contact seems to only serve the purpose of fucking with us for fun or to support a genetic crossbreeding program, utilizing our heartier traits to enhance some of their own weaker species before we go extinct. These races could extract the same material from Franklin's people, but due to their being protected by their adoptive races, they are exempt from involuntary meddling. There is apparently a very complex hierarchy among these races and a lot of crossbreeding involved. These sorts of programs usually require a treaty of some sort, but Franklin is not certain that there is really any sort of a treaty between our civilization and the race(s) that is harvesting our genetic material. There is, he says, an "unofficial" treaty called the GREADA Treaty, but it is not really being honored by the ETs. It does involve a technology-for-DNA trade-off, but the ETs have violated the agreement several times in the last fifty or so years.

It's all a bit of a blur to me now, and Franklin has since gone back to wherever he came from. I thought he was currently living in China, but I am beginning to think that was a facade. The last thing Franklin said to me as I left his hotel and went to find a taxi was that his people and ours are one and the same, we are brothers and sisters, only his side of the family was given all the benefits of our parents' teachings and inheritance. You and I, however, were left out in the wilderness to fend for ourselves. Hopefully, our well-to-do siblings will eventually come and help us before we allow ourselves to be destroyed from within by a few greedy and corrupted assholes.

The last thing Franklin said about all this was, "We are all standing on the shoulders of giants."

Afterthoughts

Before I end this, here are a few random points that I wanted to squeeze into this story but could not find the most opportune insertion points:

- Franklin also said that sound waves were used to build the Great Pyramid. Apparently, the frequency of the heavy blocks can be countered against that of the earth's gravity and lifted with little effort.
- Atlantis was a real place, and the ruins of it can still almost be seen on the northwestern coast of Africa in a region called the Richat Structure. The works of George S. Alexander and Natalis Rosen expand upon this.
- The Schumann resonance, or the electromagnetic heartbeat of the earth, has been steadily increasing since the late 1970s. It used to be so precise that the military would set their clocks by it. Franklin suspects this increase in frequency could result in a weakening of the Veil. If this is true, he suspects that this is the reason for the sudden rush to resolve the "human problem." We are not helping things with advanced DARPA projects such as the HAARP array in Alaska.
- The entities mentioned above have been occupying our world since before we were created, but our limited grasp of the

extended world has hindered our perceptions of their presence. Throughout the ages,
we have been manipulated into seeing all
sorts of strangeness, from elves, pixies, and
goblins to Bigfoot, sea serpents, and "motherships" such as the massive craft seen over
Arizona in 1997. In fact, we only perceive
what our minds can handle, and therefore,
we usually only see things that can fit into
our own imaginations. Franklin says that the
idea of "spaceships" is limited, and what we
are seeing when we see those lights in the
night sky is often something much more,
but he will not elaborate. Keep in mind
the phenomenon of negative hallucination.
In 1770, when Captain James Cook's ship
Endeavour was off the east coast of Australia,
the natives ignored it "as if it were invisible."
Some speculate that this was because the
huge ship was such a leap from the natives'
own reality that their minds just ignored it,
creating a sort of psychological invisibility as
a defensive mechanism. Perhaps when we see
some "UFOs," we are only seeing as much as
our own minds are capable of reporting to
our conscious selves?

CHAPTER 7

Negative Influences and the Lower Frequencies

I was just thinking today about how all forms of life in our realm will fight for survival. This would seem to indicate that being alive as a tick on a rat is preferable to death. Yet you know my feelings about death, so why does it seem so important to stay on if life is miserable? Simply put, because you aren't done with the lessons yet, lessons that will greatly benefit you in the long run (and man, is it a long run!). Death is the end of a lesson, and a good student does not skip out on a lesson. Not the lessons of the greatest teacher ever: God. You die when you are finished and not before. So as they used to say on *Game of Thrones*, what do we say when we meet death? "Not today." Eventually, that day comes for us all, but we should not give in if we truly want to learn everything we can. Many of us, if not all of us, contemplate suicide at some point in our lives. I know that I did. To quote lyrics from Pink Floyd (because I always think of their album *The Final Cut* when I think back on this dark moment of my life): "I raised the blade in trembling hands, / prepared to make it but… / just then the phone rang. I never had the nerve to make the final cut." At that moment, the higher consciousness said to me, *Let's just assume you did it. Takes the pressure off, doesn't it? You're dead. Now you can just stick around and see how your life turns out.* I killed myself hypothetically that day, and I got to live out the rest of my days so far with very little suffering. And I have been very fortunate. I didn't get everything I wanted in life, of course. I'm not rich. I'm not popular.

I don't think of myself as handsome or successful by any accepted definitions. But I ain't dead. And I have a relatively easy life. Sure, I'm alone (like any good meditative monk), and I don't own any fabulous possessions (again, monkish), but I'm not unhappy. I have good family and friends, a warm home with a roof over my head, and plenty of (perhaps too much) food on my table. And even more than that, I have been able to travel more than most people, and I have seen and experienced some incredible things. Sometimes the greatest success is a digital watch lying on a wet street. I recall as a child, I saw the rat race, I saw how people struggled so hard to make it through life, and I did not look forward to it. I made myself a promise. I said I was either going to be very rich or very poor, but I would be free and happy. And I have kept that promise. And as I said, I ain't dead yet. Poor, sure, but dead? Not today.

So yes, I am able to maintain a largely happy, positive existence, and I can try to put as much positive energy as I can afford into our world by trying to help every troubled soul I see. From helping a student pass an important TOEFL exam to saving a worm from drying up on a hot sidewalk, I do what I can. Why is this important? Because we are constantly under attack from the negative, lower frequencies of fear and hate. If you haven't noticed already, this is going to get repetitive.

As I keep saying, this is a world of frequencies. All matter is energy, and on a subatomic level, that energy is vibration. How we vibrate determines the kind of energy we are, make, and attract. The kind of energy we trade in (absorb and produce) affects our reality. Lower, or negative, frequencies bring us down to lower levels, like tuning our radio to the lower AM stations, where it's all crappy talk and religion and shit. Positive, or higher, frequencies get us up to where the good music is.

The concepts of "heaven" and "hell" exist as the concepts of the highest and lowest frequencies. Sadly, where our world is now, is *very* close to the hell end of the spectrum. That's why there is so much suffering and evil in our world—it's bleeding through from the lower frequencies. I think of this whenever I see sad stories of little children getting hurt or of sad, lonely old people.

I saw two things recently. One was a little girl in Korea whose father is American and her mother is Korean. Due to her father's DNA, she is noticeably bigger than the other little girls in her pre-school class, and this causes her to be shunned a bit by her fully native classmates. Halloween is a new tradition here in Korea, and it has grown in popularity from the western English teachers who pass out candy to their students who wear costumes to their classes. The Korean parents thought the idea of their youngsters in costumes was adorable, so in Seoul, they've designated a park where the wee tots can go in their costumes and collect candy with their friends. I saw a video of this adorable little girl, dressed in the cutest little big bad wolf costume, carrying her little plastic pumpkin around to get candy, and all the other children would move away from her. All the other wee tots were playing together in their costumes, trading candy, as their parents recorded videos for posterity. This bigger little girl only had her parents, and while she was happy to get candy, you could tell she was hurt that she wasn't fitting in with her peers.

It may seem like a little thing, but it almost broke me, and again, I asked myself why we humans—all of us—have this capacity for accepting even the smallest cruelty. It's not as if the other children were beating her up and taking her candy, but she was left out none-theless, and that hurts too. It breaks hearts.

The other thing was at the other end of the age spectrum. It was a note someone had posted on their social media feed that had been written by an isolated old woman, ninety years old, who had no one in her life. The note was left at her neighbor's door, asking if her neighbor would be her friend. It said, "I am so lonesome and scared." No one should ever feel like that at any age. Thank the frequencies that her neighbor was a kind woman, and she and her daughter paid the old woman a visit and they have since become friends. But think of all the old people out there in that same awful situation who have no one and no way of reaching out.

This is the evil seeping into our world. And evil begets evil. These negative energies create more negative energy, and it grows exponentially. Sure, we see evil on a perceptively larger scale every day, but it's all the same toxic, negative shit. Big evil creates small evil that only grows. It's reproduction on a cosmic scale—as above, so below.

Certain spiritual teachers knew this, and they taught their people about these dangers. They try to keep this awareness in our consciousness, and we call this the Christ consciousness. As I have said, Yeshua was an embodiment of this consciousness, and Yeshua was actually in the priesthood of Melchizedek, as was John the Baptist before him, and Siddhartha (Buddha) was also a Christ consciousness. Before all of them was Enoch, Enki/Osiris, Thoth—there have been *many* Christ consciousnesses. Sadly, these older teachings get lost or turned to dogma, and people just believe out of ritual and *hearsay-heresy* rather than knowledge. They do not bother to study these old teachings. Those right-wing evangelical self-professed "Christians" in the US today are the worst, and they should fear a return of the Christ. They'd be some of the first to get their comeuppance. They need a new script and an education with it.

When I think of evangelicals, I think, "Fuck them, they deserve it." But then my frequency drops. That's how it works. Anger, hate, fear—these are the negative energies. They allow more negative energies into our world, and they bring the entirety of this reality down. Ever heard old hippies say, "You're bringing me down, man"? Well, there's a reason people use expressions like that. The world is fluid energy, and where it goes is determined by that energy, whether it is uplifting to a more peaceful, loving utopian world where everyone gets the emotional sustenance they need to stay well, or whether it is from the more negative side, causing dis-ease in the collective. Right now, we are sinking into dis-ease, disharmony with our true selves. We are very close to the hell frequencies, and we are seeing it reflected in our world, in all the suffering we are seeing around us, and we see it more and more over political bullshit and religious bullshit.

We all know politics today are just plain evil no matter how you look at them, but religion is also not a good thing and has been corrupted. Much of it is based on good ideas, good teachings, but no one takes the time to learn where they came from or why they were taught in the first place, and we end up with the dogma, and we get hateful, judgmental evangelical types who bring in more negativity by making others angry, hateful, or fearful.

Have you ever thought it strange that the books of the Bible often describe people as being hundreds of years old? This is because, back then, our world was in a higher frequency, and our bodies were able to rejuvenate more effectively. Also, our genes were not encoded to degrade so rapidly as our creators had intended us to live longer until they realized they might not want us to live at all. Another possible explanation for this incredible longevity is that the people then likely ate better food than we do today as it was probably provided by these higher entities. All the processed junk we eat today, full of preservatives, artificial sweeteners, and sodium nitrate, it's poison. In the Dark Ages, human life expectancy dropped to its lowest point—and we are heading into a new Dark Age, thanks to modern organized religion and other stupidity.

Let's consider water. Water is fluid, and it is very mystical and mysterious, just like our reality. Despite its commonplace role in our day-to-day lives, scientists still don't understand all its quirky little properties. For example, why does it expand whether heated or cooled? Why does hot water freeze faster than cold water? We aren't even really sure of where our planet's water came from or why it is liquid at room temperature. As mathematician John Russo said, "It's almost like water is trying to hide its secrets." And we are, what, 70 percent water? It speaks to our world in that water seems to have its own form of consciousness. If you are not familiar with the work of Dr. Masaru Emoto, look into it. Basically, what he did was treat water with emotions, both positive and negative. Some water he labeled with words like "love" and "admiration" and "kindness." He had people project positive emotions at it or played music for it. For other water, he did the opposite. He abused water. When the water was frozen and the ice crystals examined, the positively treated water froze into beautiful, geometrically perfect shapes. The negative water looked disformed and chaotic. They've had similar results with rice.

Even more interesting, scientists in Germany have recently discovered that water has memory. According to an article from Resonance Science.org, dated October 15, 2018,

A scientific experiment was carried out whereby a group of students were all encouraged to obtain one drop of water from the same body of water, all at the same time. Through close examination of the individual droplets, it was seen that each produced different images.

A second experiment was then carried out where a real flower was placed into a body of water, and after a while a sample droplet of the water was taken out for examination. The resulted produced a mesmerizing pattern when hugely magnified, but all of the droplets of this water looked very similar. When the same experiment was done with a different species of flower, the magnified droplet looked completely different, thereby determining that a particular flower is evident in each droplet of water.

Through this discovery which shows that water has a memory, according to scientists, a new perception of water can be formed. The German scientists believe that as water travels it picks up and stores information from all of the places that it has traveled through, which can thereby connect people to a lot of different places and sources of information when they drink this water, depending on the journey that it has been on.

This has even been compared to the human body, of which each is incredibly unique and has an individual DNA unlike any other. Whilst the human body is made up of 70% water, conclusions could be drawn from these new discoveries that human tears can hold a unique memory of an individual being, through the body's store of water hosting a complete store of information that is linked to individual experience. Suggesting that everyone is globally connected by the water in the human body which travels through ongoing journeys, *whereby information along the way is always stored.*

Considering how much of our physical selves is water, it speaks volumes as to the power of thought over our physical existence. The food you eat is also mostly water, so it is important to consider the power of praying before eating. Based on these findings, the act of "saying grace" could actually have scientific merit. Speaking positive, hopeful words over food before you consume it, making it a part of your physical body, could have its benefits. So before you eat that hamburger, tell it you love it! Honestly, a plant-based diet is probably better as animals tend to be full of negative emotions when they are slaughtered, especially factory-farm animals. Those places should be shut down—they are an abomination. When you eat meat from those animals, you are ingesting all that fear, pain, and misery. You don't want that in your system.

What was I saying? Ah, yes, the negative influences.

These negative influences prey upon our very way of thinking, as they know that thought affects reality. The Nazis were big on this, turning the word "propaganda" into such an ugly concept that the father of advertising, Edward Bernays, had to rebrand it as "public relations." You should check out the works of Edward Bernays. He took the ideas of his uncle, the famed neurologist Sigmund Freud, and turned them into consciousness-altering gold. There is a fascinating documentary about it entitled *The Century of the Self.* But getting back to the Nazis and their attempts at mind control, or as they called it, *Bewusstseinskontrolle,* Nazi scientists conducted experiments in trauma-based mind control on prisoners of war and, of course, Jews. And despite most mainstream reports, they met with some success. Such so that the American government put some of the "reformed" Nazi scientists they brought over under Operation Paperclip to work continuing this research. It became known in the US as "MKUltra," the MK coming from the German spelling for mind *kontrolle*. Look it up, it's a very real and officially documented program. There are many indications that famous assassins in recent history, from Lee Harvey Oswald and Sirhan Sirhan to Mark David Chapman and John Hinkley Jr. may have been products of this program. When Chapman shot John Lennon, he said he kept hearing a voice in his head repeating the command "Kill him!" After he fired the shots, did he run away from the crime scene like a guilty person? No. He calmly placed the gun on the sidewalk and sat and waited for authorities to arrive. Both Chapman and Hinkley were in possession of copies of J. D. Salinger's novel *The Catcher in the Rye*. Hinkley's copy was found in his hotel room after the assassination attempt on Reagan. He stated that he was an admirer of Chapman's and had studied his killing of Lennon.

Although the CIA may have made strides in perfecting this method of programming assassins, no one comes close to the Israeli Mossad. Their efforts showed that mind control is best achieved by breaking the subject through prolonged periods of sleep deprivation, poor nutrition, and stress. Now consider how most people in industrial nations subsist today. In the USA, the cost of living continues to go up while the average salary stagnates. Health care is not considered a right, as it should be. Many people must work two or three jobs just to survive. And the news media keeps them stressed with continuous reports of terrorist threats, impending war, famine, pestilence, social unrest, you name it. And lord knows the food most people consume is not exactly healthy. Healthy foods, organic foods, are expensive, and not affordable to the majority of Americans. It sure sounds to me like a mass program of prolonged sleep deprivation, poor nutrition, and stress.

The idea that this is a "physical" world is an illusion as we are merely colliding with particles that are vibrating at our own frequency, creating the illusion of a corporeal world. We can see these with our eyes, but really, everything we think of as "reality" is just a mental projection inside our own skulls. We're not really seeing the full, true world that exists outside our heads. Evil influences want to bring everyone down to their level because they are just miserable sumbitches, and now that they have a strong influence on our shared reality, they are controlling how we think and feel about our world. Using mass media, they fill our heads with negativity. Some people will even try to blame it on other people right here with us—turning on ourselves. It's not really any group of us—it's these negative frequencies and the entities that reside in them. They reach out to those prone to negativity, like certain right-wing evangelicals or power-mad elites who have allowed their mentalities to become so warped by these outside influences that they would sell us all out if they thought it would get them the power to control everything. Sure, call me "new-agey" and an "old hippie," but the science is starting to prove me right. It's the same old time-tested strategy of divide and conquer.

Yes, there are other entities out there in the spectrum that are not always visible to our eyes. As we lower ourselves closer to the hell frequency through our mass negativity, we are seeing more of the evil ones—shadow people, "black-eyed kids," and various other demonic forms. You will also notice we are getting fewer reports of faeries, pixies, and angelic forms. So watch your vibes, people. Don't let the assholes bring you down. Don't let these negative influences tell you to fear perceived threats based on nothing. So-called Christian evangelicals and the emerging Q-Cultists are just as bad as any other religious zealotry—they have their own Sharia law, the very thing they fear so much. Every religion has that dogma, and they all have those zealots. Those assholes are hellbound. All of them. Don't join them. They probably started with the best of intentions, but along the way, they lost sight of the light and became corrupted by these negative forces. Remember the *real* threat is the negative energy those zealots are promoting, always blaming the Other based on perceived differences in race, religion, nationality, or creed. Honestly, what *would* "Jesus" do? Would he hate your neighbor for being Muslim? Would he scorn the homosexual? Would he kick out the immigrant seeking refuge for their family after his government destabilized their government and turned their neighborhood over to some local warlord?

Fuck no. *There is room for everyone.* If you don't agree with someone else's choices, love them anyway. Fuck your superiority complex.

I have said this before, and I will say it 'til I die. *Two rules*, people.

1. Never hurt any other sentient being, either physically or emotionally. When you do (and you will, we are human and we make mistakes), apologize.
2. Never enforce your opinions, ideologies, or beliefs on anyone else. Share them, discuss them, learn from them but never enforce them. Live as you choose and let others do so as well.

That's it. Anything that doesn't violate those two rules, have at it. Or as all the Teachers have always said and yet we still ignore, do unto others as you would have them do unto you. Be nice. You don't have to love everything, but for the sake of the heavenly frequencies, *be nice* and not that fake, judgmental "nice" the evangelical types puke up with a side of perceived superiority. Be genuinely nice. Seek the truth—don't believe the bullshit the negative-owned media is promoting, trying to instill more fear into you. (Example: no, schools are not teaching children to be pansexual. But do watch your schools for any other indoctrination outside the Two Rules.)

Admittedly, in large part, the media is to blame. And they do it consciously, out of a need to sell the products and programs of their sponsors. Have you ever noticed how many adverts there are for alcohol and pills? They fill your thoughts full of dis-ease, pollute your food and water, and then sell you the cure. But it's not really a cure. It comes with a slew of side-effects that you will also have to pay to treat. It's an endless poisonous cycle. Take cholesterol medication as an example. Most of it is terrible for your body. Don't take a pill. Change your diet. Adopt a plant-based meal plan. You can still eat all the crap you love one day out of the week, and your body—and you—will feel so much better. Don't buy into the Big Pharma plan. Remove your mind from it.

I'm not saying all medication is bad. As I mentioned, I take medication to control my blood pressure. And vaccines are not going to make your children autistic. We do need a more thorough vetting system at the Food and Drug Administration, however, one that is based on health and human well-being rather than corporate kick-backs. And at the risk of sounding even crazier, I do question the addition of fluoride to the water supply. It is a toxin with many deleterious effects that have been documented in numerous studies. It fits in with lead, mercury, and other poisons that cause chemical brain damage—just the thing for dumbing down a population.

Be careful not to take anything you don't really need and read the fine print. Advertisers don't care about your well-being—they want your money. The pharmaceutical industry wants you to stay sick because they want your money too. And above it all, there are unseen factions that want to reduce the human population. And there are several factions among us playing right into their hands. Once again, it's the old divide-and-conquer method that never seems to fail as the talking heads on the screens vie for influence and pit us one against the other. Certain people in the US government got rid of the fairness doctrine, the law that once insisted on fairness and truth in broadcasting in the USA, and then they destroyed our educational system and dismantled our critical thinking skills. This was no accident. Now we have hateful idiots like Tucker Carlson spouting vileness to the masses, and we have legitimized expressions like "alternative facts" and "fake news," and we are at each other's throats. Be nice, seek truth, fuck fear. That's what the Christ would do. Anyone who does otherwise is not a Christian. It's that simple. Raise the frequency, folks. Let's stop turning on each other and tune in that heaven we've been hearing so much about.

Rise above it.

CHAPTER 8

Are You Still Here?

Well, look at you, hanging on like the tenacious bronco buster of in(s)ane information that you are! I am impressed. Good for you for having an open mind and patience. The patience of a saint. Well, if you've come this far, let's go a little further. Allow me to bring the crazy. (This is fun. It sure beats screaming it on a street corner. People throw their lattes at me and then the police tell *me* to leave! I mean, where am I supposed to get a license to rant like a loon in public? Where did Donald Trump get his?) All right, here we go for another deep dive. Once more unto the breach, as King Henry said.

The moon is hollow! It's an artificial satellite, put in place to regulate the tides of our planet to restabilize it after some distant cosmic cataclysm threw it off-balance, perhaps the very same cataclysm that tilted it on its axis by 23.5 degrees and screwed up our well-decorated former equator. Indeed, ancient peoples around the world spoke of a time "before the moon," describing a night sky that lacked the big white friendly face we now gaze upon romantically. The moon keeps our ocean tides regular, and it also tends to screw with the tides of our own brain chemistry a bit. I'm sure you're aware of the etymology of the word "lunatic." (Please, hold your jokes until after the presentation.)

While many planets we have discovered also have moons (usually more than just the one), our moon is strangely unique. For one thing, it is set at such a precise distance between the earth and the sun that it perfectly blocks out the sun during an eclipse. That is mathematically remarkable. In fact, it is a 1/1,000,000,000,000 chance.

No other moons we have seen hold such a seemingly specific place. Also, the moon's rotation exactly matches its orbit in a way we call "tidal lock" so that we only ever see the one side. Before the development of our modern space programs, the so-called dark side of the moon had been hidden from our prying eyes. Imagine you are walking toward someone and as you pass, they turn to make sure you only see their front. Wouldn't you suspect they were hiding something from you behind their back? Or am I just paranoid? We will get to the oddities spotted on that side of things later. For now, let's look at the basic structure of the moon.

Our moon is millions of years older than the earth, so that throws the earth-collided-with-another-celestial-object theories into doubt. And as for the idea that the moon was just passing by and got caught in earth's gravity well, that theory does not hold up when we consider the size of our moon and its near-perfect geocentric orbit. Our moon is not proportional to our planet as other natural satellites around other planets are. If it were, it would only be thirty miles across. Instead, it is seventy-two times larger. That's a quarter the size of the earth itself. Even if such a massive object were just naturally caught in our gravity well, it would have developed a wildly elliptical orbit, one that extended a bit beyond a geocentric orbit as it passed and was gradually pulled back. Our moon does not have such an orbit. Instead, it remains roughly the same distance from the earth during its entire trip around. The earth's rotation should, by all known physics, be throwing the moon into a furious counter spin, and yet there it sits, like an unblinking eye in the sky. In fact, if you view a full eclipse from space, the antumbra around the moon gives it the appearance of a gigantic eye with the moon as its pupil. Also, most natural satellites orbit their planets around the equator, but our moon orbits at a tendency of five degrees—the exact distance, elevation, elliptical course, and speed to create tidal flow and seasons.

A lot of conspiracy theorists claim that humans never made it to the moon, and they cite old photographic images in which the light source doesn't seem to match what would exist on the moon, odd lines appearing in some of the photographs, etc., to support this theory. I do not fully support their claims as I am convinced the official account of the moon landing is true. They present these allegedly fake photographs and alleged suggestions from acclaimed director Stanley Kubrick that he assisted in producing a film of a fake moon landing. Apparently, Kubrick put several clues in his film adaptation of *The Shining* to turn it into a sort of visual confession, much to the anger and dismay of the book's author, Stephen King. For example, they claim Kubrick changed the number of the most-haunted room at the Overlook Hotel from room 217 to room 237 because 237 is the mean distance from the earth to the moon (a simple Google search will show that this is not exact, however). There is also the scene in which Danny is playing with his toy cars when a ball rolls to him, seemingly from nowhere. He slowly stands, rising while wearing a sweater depicting the Apollo 11 rocket, suggesting a reference to the launch of the rocket that first took humans to the moon. Curiously, the pattern on the carpet on which he is playing is one of hexagons. And there is the appearance of the spooky twin girls, who do not appear in the novel. This is said to be a reference to the Gemini space program. The film is also loaded with a few not-so-subtle jabs at King himself, as Kubrick and King became enemies as a result of Kubrick's changes to the original story. The two of them remained enemies until Kubrick's death in 1999. However, if you read the book and watch the movie version of the sequel to these literary and cinematic works, *Doctor Sleep*, I must say I was very impressed with how director Mike Flanagan reconciled these artistic differences. This is not related to anything other than I like to call out good work when I see it.

So what was I talking about? Ah, yes. M-O-O-N spells "moon!" (Another Stephen King reference. Get it? I'm sorry, I really like Stephen King's work.) Anyway, I am betting any faked images or film were part of a plan B put in place by the US government. The Space Race was all the rage in 1969, and the Soviet Union had a commanding lead. If the moon landing had failed, it would have been a tremendous embarrassment for the United States. Therefore, it would make sense that they would have a backup plan—a fake landing to present to the world should disaster befall the real astronauts. Perhaps some of the images from the fake version got leaked along with the actual pictures and footage? Either way, good fortune shined on our astronauts, and they made it there and back again safely. The reasons I believe this are as follows: (a) come on, seriously? and (b) if it were fake, why would they leak an account of the first astronauts reporting large spacecraft on the surface of the moon? Indeed, this is what reportedly happened when Neil Armstrong switched from the public channel to the emergency medical channel to report, "They're here. They're parked on the side of the crater. They're watching us." Indeed, there were two full minutes when there was no public trans-mission from the lunar surface and body language experts note that upon their return to the earth, the astronauts did not carry them-selves like men who had just had the amazing experience of being the first on the moon. They looked sullen and had trouble facing the cameras like they had a major secret that they could not reveal. In the years since, many astronauts, including Buzz Aldrin, have spoken out about seeing extraterrestrial craft on various space missions. It's no wonder they get so angry when people accuse them of faking the landing.

Another curiosity about our moon is the craters. Although they vary in width, suggesting objects of varying mass have struck the surface with a range of force, the craters on the moon all have the same depth. As the narrator of the video "The Moon Is Artificial, and I Can Prove It: Alien Observatory" from the YouTube chan-nel Universe Inside You describes, "When astronauts attempted to drill into the craters, they were barely able to penetrate the surface. They also discovered processed metals like brass, mica, and pure tita-nium, which are not naturally occurring elements. They are created and used for architectural design." Also consider the fact that when NASA crashed the Apollo 12 lunar module onto the moon's sur-face, their seismic devices recorded that the moon "rang like a bell" for almost forty minutes. This was such a stunning discovery that NASA decided to try it again with an even heavier rocket. Apollo 13's rocket struck with the equivalent of eleven tons of TNT. As the video narrator reports, "Even though the seismic equipment was over one hundred miles from the crash site, according to NASA, this time the moon 'rang like a gong' again, reverberating for three full hours within the two-kilometer radius of the landing." Now imagine, if you were an ET stationed inside the moon for these seismic tests, how pissed off would you be?

The video continues:

> In 1970, after years of research, two Russian scientists, Vasin and Shcherbakov, published an article in Sputnik magazine titled "Is the Moon Creation by Alien Intelligence?" Translated, it theorized that the moon is "an artificial Earth satellite put into orbit round the Earth by some intelligent beings unknown to ourselves." Based on the sheer logic of its perfect size and orientation, they believed the moon was placed in the Earth's orbit ages ago. And they're not alone. In 2006, after decades of research, two Brits, Knight and Butler, also published their research in a book titled *Who Built the Moon?* They pointed out that the absolute perfectly proportional geometry and the sequencing of integers for every aspect of the moon was duplicated by no other body in the solar system. They also discussed the huge but ultra-light mass. In the end, they created a very persuasive conclusion, stating, "If higher life only developed on Earth because the moon is exactly what it is, and where it is—it becomes irrational to cling to the idea it is a natural object."

God help me, here comes the math again. Yes, the moon, like the Great Pyramid of Giza, appears to carry mathematical and geometric information. These numbers are so precise, I am told, that it boggles the mind. As one NASA scientist Robin Brett put it, "It seems easier to explain the non-existence of the moon than it does to explain its existence." These numbers are also featured in the video "The Moon Is Artificial, and I Can Prove It: Alien Observatory." They can also be confirmed by some digging on other websites, including NASA.gov.

There are also several reliable accounts of artificial structures being found on the moon. In the 1970s, the CIA's Stargate Project at the Stanford Research Institute had remote viewers target specific coordinates on the dark side of the moon. They reported detecting ET bases consisting of spherical buildings, towers, and other massive structures. William Cooper, a former Navy intelligence officer, claims he was shown photos taken by the Apollo astronauts that clearly showed these bases, as well as massive "motherships." Even before we had lunar orbiters, backyard astronomers have been reporting strange lights, craft, and bridge-like structures on the moon's surface since the invention of the telescope. The continued official "silence" has earned a mocking alternative meaning for the acronym NASA: "Never a Straight Answer."

But enough about the moon. Once again, you can easily conduct your own research based on the information in these pages and a quick hop around the internet. Will my information always prove to be 100 percent accurate? Most likely not. However, you will find that there is more than enough substantiated evidence to support a very strong legal case against the official stance of "We have no evidence of an extra- or ultraterrestrial presence on or around this planet or any other." And should the videos I mention here ever be removed from the internet, don't worry. I have copies. And I'm sure many others do as well.

I don't know about you, but for me, images of the moon always conjure up memories of camping trips. I love to go camping. And a big part of camping is stories told around the campfire. And the moon itself is rather ghostly in appearance. I mentioned earlier in the book that I might pad it out by relating my own personal ghost stories. I figure this chapter might be a fine place to do just that as it is kind of a throwaway chapter, added in as extra information for the final draft.

As I mentioned before, I am not exactly sure what ghosts actually are, whether they are indeed conscious or if they are mere echoes left on our frequency by a traumatic death event. Perhaps it is both? One story that supports the echo hypothesis was told to me by a good friend, a fellow I grew up with. He met his wife during our wild college days, and they have been happily married ever since. I was fortunate enough to be invited to their wedding, and I stayed at her family's home in New Jersey on the weekend of the wedding. Her family gave me fair warning that their house was haunted. As I believe in ghosts, this creeped me out, but my curiosity got the better of me, as did the fact that as I was a college student, I could not very well afford a hotel room for the two nights I would be in town. A free couch with a ghost is still a free couch. Fortunately, if there were any ghostly manifestations while I was enjoying their hospitality, I slept through it and have nothing to report. I did ask my friend, the lucky groom, about it afterward. He was always a very down-to-earth fellow, not one given to exaggeration or flights of fancy. He related to me an experience he'd had while staying at his then-girlfriend's house when he went down to meet her family.

Her parents are fairly liberal, and so he was allowed to stay in her bedroom with her, seeing as they were both in their early twenties at the time. He awoke in the middle of the night to the sound of her bedroom door opening, and as he watched, an old man entered the room, walked around the bed, and appeared to be rummaging through the storage box at the foot of the bed. My friend nudged his wife-to-be awake, but she refused to open her eyes. She just said, "He's a ghost. Go back to sleep." To this day, my friend is amazed to recount the story as he still can't believe what he saw.

He and I grew up together, and he never believed in ghosts until this experience. In fact, he and I used to go swimming in the indoor pool at the local university's athletic center together as children. As I said, we grew up in a small college town in North Central Pennsylvania, and we could walk safely to the campus unescorted. On the way, we usually walked past North Hall. Anyone who is from northern Pennsylvania knows about North Hall. When we were children, it was an abandoned, derelict building that rose like some Gothic monster in the middle of all the modern buildings of the campus. Before this, it had housed administrative offices and a girls' dormitory. In 2002, it was refurbished to house all the campus libraries, thanks to a grant to restore it that was bestowed when it received recognition from the state as a historical landmark.

The reason North Hall is really famous around the area is because it is said to be haunted. Every person that grew up in our town or went to that university has heard the stories or has their own story to tell. From what I know, the ghost is that of a young girl named Sarah who committed suicide in the building around the time of World War I. The building was constructed soon after the American Civil War as the dormitory for the Mansfield Normal School, a place where young women went to learn how to sew, cook, speak various languages, play the piano, and generally be good wives and entertaining hostesses for their husband's parlors and drawing rooms.

As the story goes, Sarah was a resident student who lived in North Hall in the early twentieth century. She was either jilted by her fiancé or grief-stricken upon learning of his death in the Great War, depending on the story you hear. Whatever the tragedy, it broke her heart, and she flew into hysterics, as women were apparently prone to do back then. Her fellow females that lived with her in the dormitory tried to restore her to her senses, and she eventually fell asleep in her room. Figuring she would be all right for the night, the other ladies retired to their own boudoirs. However, Sarah awoke in the night and climbed to the top of one of the building's deep open stairwells. As the building was built in rural Pennsylvania in the late nineteenth century, no elevator had been included in its construction, and so these large stairwells were the only way of moving from floor to floor. Once at the top, she threw herself over and plummeted to her death.

The school released a statement saying that a young girl had taken ill and gone home, where she had died. But the residents of the school at the time knew the truth. Soon, they began seeing Sarah's ghostly apparition wandering the halls in her white nightgown, carrying a candle that became her trademark. Sightings of this ghostly apparition continue up to the present day.

When my sister and I were children, we used to play detective. We skulked around North Hall once, as we suspected there were some *Scooby-Doo* type shenanigans afoot, obviously a cover for an international smuggling ring. One of the campus security officers stopped us to ask what we were doing, sneaking around a derelict and possibly dangerous old building. We told him our theory, and he told us that the building did, indeed, have a history but not for smugglers. He told us that in 1967, when the building was still serving as a girls' dormitory on the upper floors, two international students were staying in the building over Christmas break. The girls called campus police to report the sound of a rocking chair and a woman crying coming from one of the locked rooms. Being on the campus police force at the time, he had been one of the officers to investigate, and upon opening the locked room, found no one inside, of course. They closed the room and locked it up again, but a few hours later, the girls, now terrified, called back to report the same disturbance. They were given permission to move into a different building for the remainder of the break.

When I was growing up, it was a badge of courage among the local school children to sneak into North Hall, and of course, I had joined one such excursion. On that trip, however, we had seen nothing but trash, broken bottles, old furniture, and a lot of pigeons and pigeon poop. Two friends of mine reported that on their trip inside, they had been walking on the fourth floor, looking into the old empty dorm rooms, littered with trash, broken bits of plaster, and peeling wallpaper. One room they came across, however, was not in any form of disarray. They said it seemed to glow with a soft natural light, and it was pristinely decorated in early-twentieth-century fashion with striped wallpaper, a comfortably adorned bed, and a vanity table, at which sat a young woman casually brushing her hair. As she turned to look at them, they bolted back down the steps and out of the building, terrified. Once outside, they were met by one's little brother who had been too scared to go inside. He asked if they had been caught by the security guard. They said, "We didn't see any security guard," to which the little brother replied, "Then who was that chasing you past the windows?" They swore they would never go back inside. To this day, all three stand by their story and have not changed a single detail.

For college students during the 1970s and '80s, it was a popular place to sneak inside with your date to go "ghost-hunting" and to carry on as young college students do. There is apparently an alumnus of the university who is also a medium, and she claims to have made a connection with Sarah during her time as a student. Every year, she returns to the school and communicates with Sarah, which would indicate evidence of the consciousness hypothesis.

As children, when my friend and I would walk past North Hall on our way home from the swimming pool, I was always scared to look up at the building. I was afraid I would see the ghostly apparition of a young woman gliding emotionlessly across one of the building's open porches. It really is a beautiful building with sculpted archways, stone faces peering out from the decorative masonry, and Victorian porches where you can visualize the young women and their male suitors of the day sitting for tea in their period clothing. The salad days! The porches are still there, but now they are enclosed with large glass windows and heated, making them ideal for late-night study sessions. This makes me feel good, as I am certain that if Sarah is in there, and conscious, she is happy to have some company again.

My own story of a North Hall ghost sighting takes place around the turn of the century (God, that makes me feel old). It was 1995, and by then, I had gotten over my fear of looking at the architecture and would sometimes plant myself on a small wall nearby, gazing into the windows of the then-empty building at night. I enjoyed singing, and as it is a small campus, there was usually no one around in the wee small hours after midnight, so I would sit there, looking at the windows facing me, a few feet away, and I would quietly sing my favorite songs of the time. I am partial to ballads. I recalled reading that Sarah and the girls of her day would often gather and sing at the railings of the very stairwell from which she killed herself. At the time, I had come to feel a sort of connection with Sarah, as by then I had racked up my own share of broken hearts. I sympathized with her. We were both alone in the world, or so my melodramatic college-aged mind saw it. Some people report hearing singing in the building, sometimes the sounds of a piano, which they had back then in the music rooms on the top floor. Considering they had no elevators back then, how the hell did they get pianos up there?

One night, as I sat on the wall, gazing into the windows and singing quietly to myself, I saw a candlelight move slowly into the frame of the window on my far left. I fell silent as I watched it move down the hallway, into the windows directly in front of me. It stopped, and I could see a blurry white figure that appeared to be carrying the light. Then it drifted straight up to the window on the next floor and continued back the way it had come. My whole body was tingling. This building sits in the middle of the campus, and there is no road from which it could have been the reflection of passing headlights. I recalled reading in a book about local legends entitled *Flatlanderes and Ridgerunners*, written by local author James Glimm, that Sarah was sometimes called "The Ghost of All Floors." Since she passed through all the floors on her way down the stairwell when she died, she could move freely between them. Was this what I had seen? Had Sarah finally come to listen to me sing or perhaps tell me to shut the hell up? To this day, I wonder. Perhaps I will meet her someday, in some form or another. I do consider her a friend.

That's one of my stories that gives me my belief in the existence of ghosts, whether they be conscious or echo. My other story takes place in Raccoon Creek State Park, in the Western Pennsylvania region of Clinton County. While attending graduate school, I went with some friends to a Dave Matthews concert at the Star Lake Amphitheater in Burgettstown. We camped in the state park, setting up our tent and joining in a little tailgating before going into the show. After the concert, we went back to the campsite and failed miserably at trying to get a campfire started. It had started to drizzle a bit, and so the wood was wet. We stood there in the dark, chatting about the concert, and enjoying the cool drizzle after a night of dancing in the summer heat. As we chatted, I spotted white figures moving among the trees around our campsite. "Who do you suppose that is?" I asked. My friends followed my gaze into the dark. "Who's who?" they asked. "There!" I said, pointing. "Moving between the trees! There are like three or four people, dressed all in white! Can you see them?" They apparently could not, so I ventured out into the trees to meet whoever it was. "Hello?" I said. "Can I help you? Can you help us start a campfire?" Nothing. No sound except for the laughter of my friends. There was no one out in the dark. I returned to my friends, but a moment later, the figures were back again. I got spooked and slept in the car all night. The next morning, I woke up early (I'm tall and can't sleep in a car) and got the campfire going. We cooked some breakfast then packed up our gear and left. On our way out of the park, we stopped at the public restrooms and pavilion to freshen up. One of my friends stopped to check out some of the information posted on the board at the kiosk. "Holy shit!" she said. "Matt, come look at this!" It was a newspaper clipping, posted under the glass. The headline said, "Have you seen a ghost? Raccoon Creek State Park is said to be haunted by the ghosts of Native Americans…"

Another interesting point about this state park, the area around our campsite was covered with patches of Indian Pipe, growing under the trees. For those "in the know," Indian Pipe is also known as ghost plant because of its white color. It does not have chlorophyll and gets its energy from fungi that in turn get their energy from photosynthetic trees. I failed botany two semesters in a row, but I do know my Native American folklore. According to the Natives, ghost plant grows in abundance in places where ghosts walk. I recognized the plant immediately because it can be brewed into a tea that has very relaxing properties. When you're a Deadhead in the middle of Pennsylvania, you learn to identify anything that can produce a natural mellow.

And finally, I am not sure this one was a ghost, but it sure was weird. The very same friend who had noticed the bulletin about the ghosts of Raccoon Creek and I were driving back from a friend's house in Indiana, Pennsylvania, one night (home of Jimmy Stewart and the amazing Ninth Street Deli subs!). It was after 2:00 a.m., and the traffic lights at the intersections along the main street had been turned to flashing yellow caution lights. This is common in small towns as there isn't enough traffic in the wee small hours to warrant the full green-yellow-red progression. Being a cautious driver, my friend slowed to a stop at one intersection. As we sat there, something moved across the street directly in front of us. Based on descriptions I have read, I would say this was one of the so-called Shadow People that have been getting a lot more notice in the paranormal circles these days. The best way I can describe it was a dark figure, blurred in a way similar to the predator's camouflage in the *Predator* film series.

I watched it move silently under the streetlights and disappear into the darkness on the other side. I said aloud, "What the hell was that?" and my friend gasped and said, "You saw it too?" Indeed, I had. I asked her what it had looked like to her. She described the same blur but said that it was shaped like a person wearing a cape. To me, it had just been a blur. I wish I had had the wherewithal during the sighting to roll down my window and try to yell at it, instigate communication with an informal, "Hey, what the hell are you?" But then considering what I have read about dark entities like this, perhaps it is best that I was stunned into silence.

So there they are—my pad-the-book ghost stories. Again, I must apologize for my scattershot writing style. This chapter goes from the moon to ghosts to the moon again! Why the moon again? Because it was John F. Kennedy that kicked off the initiative to get our species to the moon, and it is John F. Kennedy that I would like to talk about now.

CHAPTER 9

Oh My God, They Killed Kennedy! You Bastards!

Throughout this work, I have warned of the lower-frequency entities that are at work in our world to drag us down into their hellish realities. Why are they doing this? They want to enslave us. Misery loves company. They want to feed on our energy. Take your pick. Who are they, and how are they doing this? The twentieth century was a time of great progress for these evil entities, largely due to the emergence of mass communication. The history of the United States of America, a nation conceived in noble concepts like liberty and freedom and equality (for what their primitive notions of such a thing as "equality" represented, anyway) has taken a very dark and sinister turn toward the advancement of this evil agenda. For this, I will add this entry to discuss one of their biggest moves. It started in 1933 and culminated in two significant murders in 1963 and 1968. Before you read my wackadoo theory, let me restate for the record, could I be wrong? Of course. But check my information. I only include this bit as a warning of how these forces operate.

Thoughts on the Kennedy Assassinations

Well, you've reached that age when you start asking some of the hard questions. Which universities should I apply to? What do I want to do with my life? And Who killed the thirty-fifth president of the United States?

As you may have heard, I have conducted extensive research into this particular topic, and many others related to the ideas that have become the subject of conspiracy theory—now a wholly recognized field of academic study. Incidentally, I wrote my master's thesis on this topic, entitled "Conspiracy Theory as Literary Theory." However, before I get into the details of this particular conspiracy, it is important to recall one thing: conspiracy theories can be dangerous. It is a slippery slope around the so-called rabbit hole of conspiracy theory. If you do not do your due diligence and keep a healthy amount of skepticism in your inquiries, you run the risk of going over to the dark side, and the next thing you know, you're ranting online like yet another deluded individual (Q) now threatening the fabric of our democracy with cultlike devotion to a messy labyrinth of grade A cuckoo. So keep your wits about you.

Having said that, I would be remiss if I did not say that I completely disagree with the idea pushed by the mainstream that the phrase "conspiracy theory" is equivalent to "crazy bullshit." This is dangerous Orwellian doublespeak. Take it from a student and sometimes teacher of literature that the word "Orwellian" is often misused by people to mean anything "authoritarian." That's too broad a concept for this delicate terminology.

Orwellian actually refers to the very *language* that shapes our thoughts and dictates how we think about things. Saying conspiracy theory is the same thing as crazy bullshit is very Orwellian. It is alarming how often we are seeing this today. Opposing viewpoints are now "fake news." Lies are now "alternative facts." And whistleblowers are now "enemies of the state." Modern English is loaded with examples of Orwellian doublespeak, and it goes back a lot farther than Trump and Fox News.

In short, conspiracies exist. They exist at almost every major turn of human history.

They are as real as math and science, but no one ever rolls their eyes when you talk about a mathematical theory or a scientific theory. However, as with all theories, conspiracy theories can be dangerous if not exposed to the full light of skepticism and thorough vetting. There are crazy conspiracy theories, just as there have been crazy mathematical and scientific theories although there have admittedly been a lot crazier from the conspiracy field.

Having said all that, let's get to the meat of the question: *Who do I think killed John F. Kennedy?* Short answer: Not Oswald. Do I think there were a conspiracy and a cover-up? Yes. Yes, I do. If I had to name one person that was likely instrumental in the killing? George Herbert Walker Bush.

And now on to the detailed answer. I had intended this to be a short essay. However, I am long-winded, and I like to write, so I apologize in advance. Also, keep in mind that this is just my opinion. I could be wrong. Nonetheless, this is what I currently think happened. New information could always change my mind.

To really understand why people suspect there was more to the JFK assassination than the "official story" handed out by the Warren Commission, you have to go back to 1933 and a little-known conspiracy called "The Business Plot." As far as I recall, they do not teach you about this in middle-school history classes, and this raises a big red flag to me as it seems like something every American student should learn about, even as just a cautionary tale.

The Business Plot was an "alleged" attempted coup to overthrow the presidency of Franklin D. Roosevelt. It was started as a reaction to a perceived threat to the burgeoning investment banking industry in the United States. Investment banking really blossomed in the nineteenth century following the Civil War when a lot of currency brokers and mercantile firms became private banks. The distribution of wealth immediately started to show a heavy imbalance favoring these emerging money-movers, and the stock market crashed, leading to the Great Depression. When FDR came out with his New Deal, he established the Glass-Steagall Act, which separated investment banking from commercial banking, making us all safe from the machinations of bankers using the money of private individuals in shady, often risky investments. The bankers didn't like this as it made their plans of mega-wealth more difficult. So they organized a fascist veteran's group to overthrow FDR's government and establish their own business oligarchy. They selected Retired Marine Corps Major

General Smedley Butler to act as their would-be puppet dictator.

Major General Smedley Butler was a good American, however, and after attending a few meetings with the conspirators' contacts, he ratted out the lot of them to the federal government. However, as the depth of the conspiracy came to light and the names of certain people involved turned out to be top contributors to the economy, it was agreed that prosecuting the men behind the plot could be harmful to that all-important economy. The phrase "too big to fail" rings a bell, or "too big to prosecute," as they said in 2006 when a lot of big banks were bailed out and no one was ever prosecuted for the mismanagement of hedge funds leading to the housing collapse that caused the recession of that year.

Long story short, the whole thing was chalked up to an embarrassment that could not be foisted upon America's wealthiest financiers, so the whole thing was swept under the rug and they used the media that they owned—already wielding a powerful influence on public opinion—to sell it as a hoax that was ridiculed and quickly forgotten. To this day, it is referred to as an "alleged plot." That word, "alleged," is a very important word.

The men behind the plot were allowed to go back to controlling the US economy, doing what they did to bring in the money. However, they were not about to give up on their plans of mega-wealth. Having failed with an overt attempt at seizing power, they decided to go covert. They spent the next thirty years infiltrating the government at all levels and departments. Their most significant achievement was the establishment of the Central Intelligence Agency in 1947, having grown out of the Office of Strategic Services (OSS), Strategic Services Unit (SSU), and the Central Intelligence Group (CIG), respectively. These men took to the intelligence game like fish to water, and they have been building it and expanding it and its powers ever since. It now encompasses a total of at least seventeen different agencies.

Once they felt they had a secure grip on the information agencies (they owned the mainstream media in the US, and now they were securely in control of whatever "official stories" came out of the government itself), they made their move on November 22, 1963, and Kennedy never made it home from Dallas.

There was a flurry of activity and odd behavior that exploded on that day in Dallas, a lot of which does not make sense, some of which flies in the face of the Warren Commission's official findings. It all comes together to form a seemingly (conveniently?) impassable smoke screen that hides the truth of what actually transpired. I can't list them all here, but here are a few key things I would like to address to support my idea:

1. There is a telling video of JFK and Jackie departing the Dallas Airport on the morning of November 22. In the video, we can see the presidential limousine and the two Secret Service agents who were to jump onto riding platforms on the back bumper, where they were to act as human shields. Behind them was the Secret Service follow-up car. Just as the two agents were to jump onto the rear bumper, their director stands up in the follow-up car and calls them off. You can see

the exasperation of the agents, as they gesture with their arms as if to say, "Are you kidding me?" Ultimately, they follow orders and are not there to take any of the bullets that eventually would kill Kennedy barely thirty minutes later. At the time of this writing, you can still view the video on YouTube by searching "Kennedy bodyguards called away."

2. If you ask anyone from that era, everyone recalls where they were when JFK was assassinated—except George H. W. Bush. When asked by a reporter where he was at the time of Kennedy's assassination, he replied, "I can't remember." Interesting, when you learn that at the time, he was employed by the CIA, and CIA records place him *in* Dallas on November 22, 1963. How do you not remember that? There is even an old grainy black-and-white photo of a man reported to be him standing in front of the book depository from which Oswald was said to have fired. The photo was taken immediately after the assassination.

3. It was also interesting to see the video of Bush's eulogy for President Ford at Ford's funeral. Bush seems to laugh as he mentions the idea of "a deluded gunman" killing Kennedy. Hardly appropriate, either way. (Also viewable on the world's collection of home movies, YouTube.)

4. Events following the assassination didn't get any calmer, and the smoke screen seemed to continue for two days following, with alleged mishandling of Kennedy's body, defiance of Texas State Law in not allowing the local medical examiner near the body

before it was whisked back to Washington, DC, and agents in the follow-up car reporting smelling gunpowder on street-level and Kennedy actually yelling, "I'm hit!" before he was actually shot. Some attribute this to the first shot missing and hitting pavement beside his car, striking him with chips of asphalt. The craziest thing, however, is the assassination of the alleged assassin, Oswald, on November 24 as he was being transferred through an underground parking garage from his holding cell to the courthouse across the street. Jack Ruby, a local Dallas nightclub owner and lowlife with known connections to organized crime, took it upon himself to leap from the crowd and shoot Oswald at almost point-blank range, killing him before he could have his day in court and say what he was saying moments before he was shot ("I'm just a patsy!") on the official record. Jack Ruby had already been diagnosed with terminal cancer at the time.

So Where Did the Fatal Shot that Killed JFK Come From?

If you've seen the Zapruder film and its use in the Oliver Stone film, *JFK,* you are familiar with the "back and to the left" commentary. That is, experts who viewed the film wondered, if the fatal bullet struck Kennedy from behind, why did the impact appear to drive his head backward, like the shot had hit him from the front? Others say this was a muscle reaction from the bullet striking below the base of the skull, which would cause the head to snap back. The problem

I see with this is that the final, fatal shot showed a clear entry wound near the top of the skull, not below the base. There are several initial reports from eyewitnesses on the scene that claimed they heard shots coming from an area now commonly referred to as "the grassy knoll" on Dealey Plaza. Behind this knoll was a short fence hidden by a line of trees, and beyond that, a train yard. This would have been an ideal location for a sniper to have been waiting. Still others claim the fatal headshot came from an overpass overlooking the plaza. We'll probably never know the whole story.

Recently, a new video came to my attention that claims the fatal shot actually came from the Secret Service follow-up car—and it was totally accidental. The Secret Service car was equipped with an AR-15 rifle (the kind commonly used in mass shootings throughout the US today). According to this account, when shots first rang out, an agent in the car grabbed the AR-15 and stood up to return fire just as the driver hit the brakes. Thrown off-balance, the agent's gun arm went up, and he pulled the trigger, and the round hit Kennedy, killing him. It's an intriguing idea—that the whole thing was an accident, and the cover-up was put in place to protect the bumbling of the Secret Service. This theory has since been "debunked" (allegedly), but you can find the account online.

Moreover, in his book *Crossfire: The Plot that Killed Kennedy* (1989), journalist Jim Marrs's extensive examination of the details of the assassination, Marrs asserts that in the 1970s the rooftop of the records building beside the book depository from which Oswald is alleged to have fired was being torn up to put in a new air-conditioning system. Workers found an old, weather-pitted shell casing that showed evidence of having used a sabot slug. Sabot slugs are used to fit smaller caliber bullets into larger caliber shells (example: a 6.5 mm bullet in a 30.06 shell) A casing of this nature could produce fragments traceable to the Mannlicher-Carcano rifle alleged to have been used by Oswald.

Other Pieces

While I do think George H. W. Bush was directly involved in Kennedy's assassination, I doubt that he was actually the triggerman. That was probably some goon(s) whose name(s) we'll never know. It is curious that two years and seven months before the assassination, Kennedy gave a speech now known as his Secret Societies Speech on April 27, 1961. In it, he openly states that "we are opposed...by a ruthless conspiracy." That speech is definitely worth a watch. Surprisingly, a link to it was hard to find. It used to be on YouTube. Transcripts are available online through a Google search.

If you listen to that speech, you might also find Eisenhower's farewell address quite telling. He famously stated, "In the councils of government, we must guard against the acquisition of unwarranted influence, whether sought or unsought, by the military-industrial complex. The potential for the disastrous rise of misplaced power exists and will persist." Eisenhower made this speech on his last night as president before Kennedy took over. It was, to me, anyway, as if he were saying, "Hey, you might want to look at this. I've survived too many wars to risk my neck going after this now, but Kennedy—it's all yours!" And Kennedy took the ball and ran with it right up until Dallas.

It seems some top men in the government were aware of the threat of a coup. Keep in mind that the "military-industrial complex" Eisenhower refers to is, in my opinion, the cabal of bankers that started their push in 1933 with the Business Plot. They have made the bulk of their money on the global stage by inciting wars and rebellions and selling weapons and warriors to both sides. Their baby is the Federal Reserve Bank, established in the US by foreign banking interests that actually lend US dollars to the US for use as currency at interest. It is a centralized bank, something the Founding Fathers of the US, and Andrew Jackson, and Abraham Lincoln, were all greatly opposed to as centralized banking causes a nation to lose control of its own money. The bankers fought to have a central bank established in the US by less-than-honorable means, and in 1913, they succeeded. The founder of this central bank, Mayer Rothschild, once famously stated, "Give me control of a nation's money, and I care not who makes the laws." This is a bit of a sidetrack to the topic at hand, but you can read all about it in a fascinating book entitled *The Creature from Jekyll Island* (1994) by G. Edward Griffin. It examines the conspiracy (there's that word again!) that established The Fed as the US central bank.

Curiously, John F. Kennedy had signed Executive Order 11110 on June 4, 1963, just six months before he was killed. This order was aimed at ending the use of Federal Reserve currency.

Now if all that weren't bad enough, there's also the assassination of Kennedy's younger brother Bobby to contend with. If the assassination of JFK does not tell you something seriously dark and shady happened to the USA in November 1963, the fact that his brother met with the same fate under similar, highly questionable circumstances just five years later should be a huge red flag. Bobby was running for president with the promise of exposing all the shadowy forces behind his brother's assassination.

After the Kennedys were taken out and Johnson had escalated the war in Vietnam (which Kennedy had opposed), the new system was entrenched. As far as I can see, every president since has toed the line. They and their media machine have given the people nonissues over which to argue, to give the illusion of a choice in our elections, but the main agenda, at its core, has proceeded unabated, regardless of which party was at the helm, bringing us to where we are today—endless war abroad and social unrest at home.

And George H. W. Bush? He became the director of the CIA, and he ran for the Republican Party presidential nomination against Ronald Reagan in 1980. When Reagan won the nomination, Bush struck a deal with him that basically went like this:

BUSH. Hey, Reagan. I can guarantee your election if you make me your VP.
REAGAN. Oh yeah? How, George?
BUSH. You know those hostages in Iran?
REAGAN. Yeah, Carter has negotiated a release, so...

BUSH. Forget that. I have people through my contacts in the oil industry and CIA who can put the kibosh on that deal. This will make Carter look weak and give you a winning bump in the polls.

REAGAN. Hm. Okay!

Now the previous dialogue is pure conjecture on my part, but Iran held the hostages until after Reagan had won the election. Incidentally, Carter launched a daring helicopter rescue mission in the last months of his presidency, but the helicopters crashed in the desert in an embarrassing display of incompetence. However, the real story is that the helicopters crashed because someone had removed filters that would have kept the desert sand out of the engines. The helicopters had been checked at a desert location before setting off on their mission. A young Oliver North—a Reagan operative who became famous during the Iran-Contra scandal in the late 1980s—was at that base when the helicopters came in and had both motive and opportunity to remove the filters, foiling the rescue attempt, embarrassing Carter, and ensuring Reagan's victory. The hostages were officially released on January 20, 1981—the very day Reagan was sworn in as president.

Incidentally, Reagan was the next president to be assassinated—almost. And it happened just three months after he was sworn in. He survived but lost a lot of blood, many saying later that this basically incapacitated him as president, leading to the image of him as a doddering leader who was always napping.

Guess who would have been sworn in as the new president had Reagan died?

The man who shot Reagan was John Hinkley Jr.—a personal friend to the Bush family. On the day of the attempt on Reagan's life, in fact, Hinkley's father was having dinner with Neil Bush, one of George H. W.'s sons. Both families had connections through a shadowy figure called Mohrenschildt, a Russian "Baron" who was perhaps the closest person to—you guessed it—Lee Harvey Oswald in the years before Kennedy's assassination.

Finally, do you recall the Glass-Steagall Act that separated investment and commercial banking concerns and started this whole mess? They finally repealed it in 1999. Many economists say this is what led to the subprime mortgage scandal that created the recession of 2006–07. Just like the stock market collapse that set this in motion in the first place, it is creating a shocking imbalance in global wealth.

I am of the mind that yes, the Kennedys were killed in a coup. The result was to further an agenda, and that agenda is coming to fruition right before our eyes today. It is a plan to subjugate all the peoples of the world by moving all the money to the top one percent (as Bernie Sanders likes to say, God love him!). It's not a Republican versus Democrat thing. It's a "*wealthy elite* versus *all of us*" thing. The two political parties fomenting all the bickering are just two puppets on the arms of the same creature, using the old divide-and-conquer scheme to keep people fighting each other instead of fighting them. Their method is destabilization on all fronts: economic, political, social, spiritual…and it's happening all over the world.

It's strange to think General Wesley Clark went on the program "Democracy Now" in 2007 and talked about seeing a list just days after the September 11 attacks of seven countries the US was planning to destabilize in the Middle East— and US forces have followed it like a recipe. We went into those countries and completely destabilized them…and then just left them that way. If you do a bit of digging, you will notice a correlation between nations the US has destabilized and nations that have attempted to dump the US "petrol" dollar (i.e., The Fed money) as their reserve currency. A popular question in Conspiracy Theory is *cui bono?* (who benefits?), the sentiment being, as always, "Follow the money."

I fear that Trump was (or still is) a part of this plan. By encouraging racial and political divisions, endorsing baseless, damaging conspiracy theories, and undermining the legitimacy of our very democracy, he has only furthered this dark agenda. And Boris Johnson and his Brexit deal are doing the same for the UK. You see how history is a continuous wave of cause and effect? All this started with new banking practices in the nineteenth century following the US Civil War. And before that…? And now there are rumors of a new Civil War in the US. I really hope that it never comes to that, but I have never seen our nation so vehemently divided. And it would make a nice little package, this whole Bankers' Plot bookended neatly between two Civil Wars.

Conclusion (Finally!)

Who do I think killed Kennedy? I think a group of very wealthy people did it, establishing today's seeming oligarchy of special business interests running our government. I think George H. W. Bush was instrumentally involved on the ground, and I think a coup was successfully carried out. Now those that seized power in 1963–1968 are putting the final touches on a world of the *very poor* (masses) lorded over by the *very rich* (elite few). And the rich will get richer, and the poor will get poorer—especially as climate change moves us closer and closer to global shortages of food, water, and habitable territory.

Pretty darn bleak, isn't it? Well, as I said, this is just my opinion. I could be very wrong about all this. In fact, I hope that I am very wrong about all this. However, there just seem to be too many coincidences and connections to reject it out of hand. As the old saying goes, "Hope for the best but prepare for the worst."

Here's something else that popped into my conspiracy-addled brain. It may sound even more nuts, but consider this, all peoples of history who were enslaved, or the victims of genocide, all had one thing in common: they didn't believe it could happen until it did.

Now, of course, all this is just theory on my part, but that higher consciousness tells me this is an accurate account of events. Allegedly or no, the idea here is that this sort of thing goes beyond politics. It always does. Everything in these realms has a spiritual reverberation. These dolts that carried out this "silent coup" were played like the greedy, stupid suckers they are. I do not believe people are inherently evil. Rather, I prefer to think there are just too many who are ignorant, "dim bulbs" lacking Light, as it were. These limited fools can be led around by the nose with promises of money and corporeal illusions of power. This is what makes them dangerous, not any inherently evil soul. Yet there does seem to be a pattern. Again, remember to look at things as multilayered events. These power-lusting people get into positions of power—they remove the fairness doctrine so they can spout any nonsense in the media, and they cut funding for schools and remove critical thinking skills from an entire generation. In this way, they produce a civilization ripe for the picking and plundering by lower-realm entities. The silent coup of the Kennedy assassinations was devastating and detrimental to our collective progress, but at the time of this writing, we just had ourselves a loud, noisy, obnoxious coup. So things do not seem to be getting better. One step up, thirteen steps back. This is why we have Work to do.

CHAPTER 10

The Great Work

This chapter is just a few more thoughts about the Veil, and something that is actually so important I am amazed that I have not mentioned it until now. This "something" is the Great Work. As I have said, I do not want to fill this book with accounts of encounters with entities from beyond the Veil. All that is at your fingertips today if you have access to the internet or a library. And as I have said, if you are reading my random blathering, then you are probably already well aware of these accounts. Suffice to say, the question is not "Do you believe in extraterrestrials?" but "Are you aware of extraterrestrials? Ultraterrestrials? What do you think they want from us?" Our world governments keep telling us that there is no evidence of an alien presence ("alien" here meaning entities from beyond our world), and yet the evidence is all around us. It's like me telling you that there's no evidence that pandas exist. All you have to do to prove me wrong is look around. Especially today, in the age of the pocket TV studio, the evidence is even more prevalent so much so that these world governments are beginning to let the facade slide and they are gradually releasing more and more information. They need to gradually desensitize the populace so as to avoid panic. But really, there is nothing to panic about. If all these entities had bad intentions toward us, they would have made their move by now. By and large, they do their best to avoid us, and who can blame them? We're the bad neighborhood, the Podunk little backwater hole full of backward superstitious bumpkins of the macroverse. But we're coming along, in little pockets, here and there. And they are noticing this, and they are offering guidance where applicable. If you have made it this far in reading this book, they are probably aware of you. Maybe expect a phone call.

Regardless, here is one more account of an encounter just to get your mental juices flowing in this direction. I like this one for the analogy used. You'll see it. This is from the website Collective Evolution.com, dated July 27, 2017. It's entitled "A Fascinating Story about 'the Real Men in Black' from Ingo Swann." Ingo Swann was a talented remote viewer engaged in the US government's Black Project known as Project Stargate. This project was deeply involved in studying paranormal phenomenon. These projects continue to this day, and I am always curious as to what new developments they have made. Surely by now they must be aware that some entities are just messing with them for fun. Anyway, this particular story goes a little something like this:

> One day, [Mr. Axelrod] entered into the secured facility at Stanford, which was not an easy thing to do. He found Swann and persuaded him to leave with him. Axelrod was accompanied by two twins, who were very tall and mysterious. They dressed in the typical "cloak and dagger" intelligence agency outfit. Swann described them as "two blond-haired, blue-eyed, military-looking assistants."
>
> The four of them flew to the west coast where Swann believed it to be the Alaskan wilderness, although he wasn't certain and was told that it's best [that] he did not know. They were flying in a Learjet and found an area deep in the forest which seemed to be for their own use. They trekked a very long time.
>
> Richard Dolan, one of the world's foremost authorities on the topic of UFOs, describes the incident well in his book, *UFOs and the National Security State, The Cover-Up Exposed 1973–1991*,

so I will quote it from here on in starting on page 154:

They came to a small lake, and Axelrod said that as dawn approached, Swann would be able to see "it" through the pines. "We now wait and hope we are lucky. Say nothing, do not make any noise…they detect heat, noise, motion like mad."

Dawn arrived, and Swann saw a fog developing over the lake. This went on for five minutes, until the fog developed a luminous neon-blue color. Then, according to Swann, the color changed to an "angry purple." Axelrod and one of the twins each placed a hand firmly on Swann's shoulders while "a network of purple, red, and yellow lightning bolts shot in all crazy directions through the 'cloud.'" Swann said he would have jumped if the two had not held him down. He saw an object, almost transparent at first, but then "solidly visible over the lake." It was triangular or diamond-shaped, growing in size.

Swann, in terror and amazement, heard a strong wind moving past, rustling the pine trees so much that some cones and branches fell on them. The object then began to shoot out "ruby red laser-like beams" as it continued to grow even more in size while maintaining its position on the lake. Very quietly, one of the twins said, "Shit! They're enveloping the area. They're going to spot us."

As Swann later recalled the event, some of the red laser beams from the object were 'blasting' pine trees, and he could hear low frequency pulsations. Axelrod whispered to Swann that the beams were probably homing in on deer or other forest creatures, as they sense biological body heat. "They're sure to home in on us," he told

Swann. Just then, one of the twins literally lifted and dragged Swann away, but not before Swann noticed the water of the lake surging upward, "like a waterfall going upward, as if being sucked into the 'machine.'"

The four ran quickly and at great length, sustaining minor cuts and bruises. Eventually they stopped, breathing hard, and waited for more than thirty minutes, until one of the twins said all was clear.

Axelrod then asked Swann whether he could "sense" anything form the craft. At this point it was quite obvious why Swann was taken from his position and role at Stanford Research Institute and into this situation. It seemed that these "government" agents believed Swann could provide some detail about what was happening here and help the government with their research and interest in UFOs.

Swann burst out laughing. "You're completely nuts, Axel! I have to be calm, cool, collected and in good shape to sense anything." But Swann offered the insight that the craft was "a drone of some kind, unmanned, controlled from somewhere else." Axelrod asked him what it was doing there, to which Swann replied "Well, for Christ's sakes, it was thirsty! Taking on water, obviously. Someone somewhere needs water… so I suppose they just come and get it. You don't need to be a psychic to see that." Essentially, said Swann, "they" treated Earth as the neighborhood supermarket.

And that's the account. I like the supermarket analogy, you see. We're like the little roadside farmer's market where passersby from the big city stop to buy sweet corn. They don't want to talk to us; they don't want anything to do with us. They just want to zip by in their shiny vehicles and snag some sweet corn. But if they drive by and notice the farmer sitting there with an arsenal of nuclear bombs, they might slow down and take a gander. There are numerous reports of UFOs drawing up massive amounts of water from lakes and oceans. And let's not forget the large numbers of cattle mutilations. Cattle mutilations and crop circles are decried in the mainstream media as obvious hoaxes, but anyone who has truly studied these subjects can see that they are most definitely not hoaxes. More on that later. My thinking on this encounter is that the drone that they saw was from a lower frequency, evidenced by the way it gave off an "angry" emotion and "blasted" trees and deer.

John Keel makes note in his work about the appearance and disappearance of these objects. Numerous eyewitness accounts describe craft becoming visible or invisible right before the eyes of the witnesses. He says the ships often glow bluish-violet or red before vanishing form sight, indicating that they are passing through our visible spectrum. They vanish above the infrared or below the ultraviolet wavelengths, but they are still there. We just can't see them. When a UFO is seen by one of us *mehumes* (mere humans, thank Robert Anton Wilson), it is likely having trouble with its cloaking mechanism, is unaware it has slipped into our visible spectrum, or is intentionally trying to be seen.

So why would such entities want to be seen? Why would they make contact in certain situations (such as the Holloman Air Force Base landing)? This plays to what I refer to as the Great Work. Remember that we are all bits of collective consciousness, akin to drops of water in a great lake. Like cells in a brain, they form synapses, synapses connect to allow conscious thought, and thereby existence (*cogito, ergo sum* as Descartes said). The Great Work is connecting all consciousness throughout the macroverse to create a universal consciousness or "God." As I said, this is reproduction on a grand scale. As above, so below. The more microminds that are connected into the macro, the more powerful it becomes, and the easier it is to create a new universal reality. This brings me back to the double-slit experiment and the Heisenberg principle (aka, the uncertainty principle).

As the double-slit experiment showed, particles such as photons are dependent on a conscious mind perceiving them for them to "become" one of any number of possibilities. I may have described this experiment before, but it bears repeating. In the experiment, physicists positioned a screen with a double-slit cut into it, facing a photosensitive cell. Then they fired one photon at the screen at a time to try to track whether it behaved like a particle or a wave. One photon should, by all our understandings of reality, have to go through one slit, or neither slit. Imagine shooting BBs through a board with two long holes cut into it. What would a surface on the other side look like after you emptied your BB supply? After sending a multitude of single photons through the slits one at a time, this would eventually result in a reflection of the two slits on the photosensitive cell, looking like I I. Instead, they got an interference pattern, which emerged like this: I I I I I I. This indicated that the photon was being interfered with, bouncing off another photon to produce this echoed effect. But there was only one photon passing through the screen at a time, so this could not be the cause. They set up a camera to record the moment the photon passed through the screen and repeated the experiment. Now they got the expected result: a simple reflection pattern of the two slits: I I. So what changed? Now the particle was being *observed* and was forced to make a choice of realities. Before, it was enacting all possible realities by going through one slit, the other slit, *both* slits, and *no* slits, all at the same time, and had been *interfering with itself* in a different possibility—a different reality! Being observed changed that, forcing it to adhere to one possibility.

It's crazy, I know, and I am bad at explaining it, so go look it up. There is an excellent video on YouTube that illustrates precisely what happened (see "Dr. Quantum—Double Slit Experiment"). My point is that our *consciousness* creates our reality as we go. Simply by observing our world, we assign a singular outcome, and it is based solely on our perception. This is why our thoughts are so important, as illustrated by Masaru Emoto's water experiments. As with the Princeton Global Consciousness Project, when all our consciousnesses sync up, we affect the very fabric of our reality.

The power of the mind is incredible, and the power of multiple minds focused on the same goal is a powerful force. The Nazis nearly used theirs to take over the world, but when the other inhabitants of the world focused their thoughts against the plans of the Nazis, they stopped them cold. And as we have discussed, the physical world is simply a manifestation of our limited understanding of the larger ethereal, or noncorporeal, world: it's an illusion. Our reality is, in fact, *all ethereal*. We, as souls, are merely here to develop in the safety of this illusory nursery, to grow our minds and become more powerful souls—souls capable of joining the outside realms of our multilayered universe, to sustain ourselves within it unfettered by these "physical" forms that we are first born into for the purpose of strengthening our true forms. We are learning to trade our physical for the psychical, and if you have been paying attention recently, you may have noticed that we, as a collective species, are starting to realize this. We are starting to collectively outgrow our nursery.

As our minds first began to develop, we became tool users. The tools allowed us to expand our creative abilities and further our thinking. This resulted in the design of more elaborate tools, and more elaborate tools developed within us more elaborate thinking. This give-and-take between the psychical and our perception of the physical continued up through the ages, and today our tools are out-performing us, forcing us to keep up by expanding our consciousness to as-yet unfathomed depths and unimagined heights. Our technology today has shown us that we can create artificial intelligence and entire artificial universes. This has led to simulation theory, which I will discuss at the end of this ride. For now, let me just say that artificial intelligence (AI) is probably not a good thing for us to be playing with right now. We could very well, at this stage, create our own overlords or worse—our own exterminators. (I added the "ex" because I don't want to get sued by James Cameron.) Thankfully, however, I don't think this is going to happen *if we can get our collective shit together.* Granted, as I have said in earlier chapters, there are factions out there that would love to see us wipe ourselves out with our own technology. But there are those other entities—the fifth column—that are trying to safely guide us to our place in the larger world. Which one we follow is up to us as individuals, on a personal level.

I am sure by now you have seen a meme containing the famous Native parable of the two wolves. The story is of a conversation between a grandfather and his grandson, and it deals with inner conflict, the battle of good versus evil for the boy's soul. The grandfather explains that the boy has two wolves fighting inside him: one wolf is anger, greed, envy, arrogance, lies, superiority, hate, fear, etc. The other wolf is joy, peace, kindness, empathy, understanding, generosity, humility, love, etc. The boy asks which wolf will win the fight, and the grandfather replies, "Whichever wolf you feed."

The negative entities are encouraging us, tricking us, into feeding the first wolf. We must remember who we are and how important all life is and only feed the second wolf. As Michael Jackson sang, you've got to start with the person in the mirror. Developing ourselves spiritually, internally, where it counts—our minds, our souls—to be good is how we win and take our place in the larger world, to take one big step toward becoming God. Each drop is a part of the lake, and the fewer polluted drops, the healthier the lake.

We mustn't allow ourselves to feel overwhelmed by all the negativity coming at us through the screens—be they Veils, TV, and laptop or our own eyes and ears. We must shut it out, at least for a few minutes each day, close our eyes, and remind ourselves of who we are, who we wish to be. Keep yourself pure inside the temples—those spots on the sides of your little skull-boat. That is, after all, why we call them temples. Words, people. They have meanings deeper than we should allow ourselves to forget. As individuals, we create the larger soul that is our species, our tribe. As the Lakota saying goes, *Mitakuye Oyasin* (all are related). I like to think that this goes beyond just people, but the first step is just getting us all to remember that we are all people. Together, we create our reality. And the key word there is *together*, so we cannot keep allowing ourselves to be fooled by their divide-and-conquer tactics. Don't let some loud-mouthed assholes with their own TV shows, political committees, or podcasts tell us who we are. We need to tell ourselves, every day. Shut out the noise and listen to the higher consciousness within. Change yourself, change the world. *As above, so below.*

You may notice I said that the photon is forced *to make a choice.* Does this mean the photon has consciousness and is somehow aware that it is being observed? The idea of panpsychism suggests that consciousness is prevalent throughout the universe and is a fundamental part of it. This is not to say that everything in the universe has consciousness, but that the basic components of consciousness exist in some form in everything. While consciousness as we generally understand it only exists in complex brains of highly evolved organisms and is defined by self-awareness, panpsychism says that consciousness is based on experience. While organisms like humans tend to have very complex experiences, organisms like bugs have very limited experiences but are still conscious in their own basic way. The idea is that consciousness can be broken down into the fundamental building blocks of reality, such as quarks and electrons perhaps, and the more these blocks come together, the more experience is possible, and consciousness derives from this. Recall in chapter 7 the article about water having memory? Water could very well have its own consciousness. The Bodhisattvas' claim that they will not move on to the higher frequencies until every blade of grass is enlightened takes on a new level of possibility. Does a blade of grass possess consciousness? Yes, if not in the way we might understand it. I bet the cells in that little blade know when the sun is shining. The basic elements are there. We know that that blade of grass, the water that nourishes it, and those of us who mow it down in its prime are all made up of the same atoms that make up everything else in the universe. Consider again the amazing fact that the atoms that make you are the same atoms that were literally forged billions of years ago and spewed forth into the universe by supernovae and that you are literally stardust. If panpsychism is correct, then your consciousness has been developing for much longer than your physical body has existed. Who knows what you have been a part of or what you may yet retain.

Speaking of consciousness and the physical form, I mentioned Nature's God earlier, and I also mention serpents and metaphors a lot in this book, for obvious reasons. Nature is full of clues to our

135

true potential. Snakes shedding their skin is metaphorical of reincarnation. A child might find a discarded snakeskin and mistake it for a dead snake when, in fact, the snake is alive and well in a brand-new skin. The transformation of caterpillar into butterfly is one of my favorite of nature's metaphors for this phenomenon. Do you think that when the caterpillar has eaten its fill and begins to build its chrysalis that it is aware of what is happening to it? Does the caterpillar think it is dying? Is it surprised to reemerge days later as a transformed being with access to a whole new dimension of its existence? Now able to fly, its perspective is greatly broadened, its awareness increased. Nature has been providing us with clues as to our own true nature since the beginning.

Of course, transformation is reflected in both the spiritual and the physical (again, *as above, so below*). As our technology develops, we are seeing it merging with our own physical forms. We will look at this more in the next chapter, but consider the recent discovery that data can be stored in DNA. Researchers are currently working on replacing our current data storage devices with DNA-based data storage. Data can be stored in the sequences of our ATC and G nucleotide chains that comprise our DNA, and it is incredibly stable and requires very little energy. This could solve a lot of our emerging data issues as our technology continues to grow by exponential leaps and bounds. But now that we know this, who's to say that our creators didn't store key information for us within all our so-called junk DNA? What if these psychical communiqués from the higher consciousness that seem to come from "elsewhere" are actually coming from within our very cellular structure? *What if the calls are coming from inside the house?*

Either way, it is all steering us on the path leading to a coming jump in our collective evolution. And it is important to remember which direction we choose to jump. This is why we have been given the task of completing the Great Work.

The Great Work is trying to sync up *all consciousness* in the collective universe (macroverse) to create an entire universe of our own design, one in which all our existential goals are met. Have you ever seen a structural comparison of the universe and the neural net-

THE BIG BLUE TURTLE

work of the human brain? A neuron in the brain bears a very striking resemblance to a galaxy cluster. Galaxy clusters unite into superclusters, which unite into even larger superclusters. The Milky Way is part of such a cluster, and you are part of the Milky Way. The human brain works because of a network of nearly seventy billion neurons that make it up. The universe is thought to have at least one hundred billion galaxies. Just as our individual conscious minds develop from the preneonatal stage on up through adulthood, coming to grips with its existence and individual identity, so too is our universe coming to grips with its own concepts of existence and identity—and each and every conscious mind within it is an active participant. Were all of us on our little planet to synchronize, harmonize as suggested by the Global Consciousness Project and other phenomena, we would literally be able to become like God and simply think our reality into existence. This synchronization is the Great Work. And yes, there is a universe inside you that created your consciousness by syncing up and so on and on and on—a fractal of consciousness. This is why the development of higher frequency thinking is so crucial. Are we to be a good witch or a bad witch? Will we be on the light side of The Force or the dark side? Will our reality be closer to heaven or hell? We cannot let ignorant, shortsighted minds full of greed, prejudice, and hate make that choice. We are a universe, a God, creating itself. When we talk together, share ideas, we are God talking to itself—we are merely meditating, making decisions, and creating our own collective identity. We are the internal dialogue of a greater being. Realizing this higher consciousness is our purpose, and it is bemusing to the higher entities and EBEs that we haven't figured this out yet.

Rise up.

CHAPTER 11

Transhumanism and Eternal Life through Science

All religions of the world promise eternal life, but none actually deliver. The teachings of the Christ do, and I am not limiting this to only Christianity. As I have said, the Christ is just an enlightened consciousness that comes around every so often to guide our progress. Christ, Buddha, Thoth...all are one. As long as they adhere to the Two Rules. Any Teacher that does not, you know that is a false prophet. In Eden, the Tree of Knowledge symbolized our entryway into eternal physical life by way of scientific development. We are starting to see that today through the exponential development of our technology. As I said, we create our own reality, and it seems anything we can imagine, we can make. Gene Rodenberry created *Star Trek* by introducing the fantastic idea of warp drive technology. Now today, we are developing actual warp drive technology that may one day be capable of carrying our descendants to distant stars to colonize Super-Earth planets. This technology will literally bend space using gravitational waves, creating huge gravity wells that will pull points A and B closer together so that traversing multiple light-years of space will be comparable to stepping over a threshold. Or it will create a gravity warp bubble that can propel a spaceship past the speed of light. I don't know, I am not a physicist. Oddly enough though, this is exactly how alleged physicist Robert Lazar allegedly described the alleged propulsion systems of the alleged alien craft he allegedly worked on at the allegedly legendary "Area 51" (Nellis AFB,

Area S4, or the Papoose Lake/Groom Lake facility). When Mr. Lazar described how these ships could "bend" space using a superheavy element that did not exist on our charts, people scoffed. Now thirty years later, not only are our scientists saying that such technology may one day be possible, but we've also found superheavy elements that fill in those once-empty spaces on our table of elements. And so to all those people who say, "Extraterrestrials can't come here! Space is too vast to traverse!" Yeah, *for us*, maybe. But even we are starting to figure it out. Just because we can't figure it out doesn't mean someone else hasn't. The Grey ETs tell us they are from a very ancient race. Where might our technology be if we survive into the next hundred thousand years? For those of us of older generations, did you ever think you would be able to sit in your car and stream a TV show on your freakin' *phone?* The people that now say such things are impossible are the same people that told the Wright Brothers that humans couldn't build flying machines. Shortsighted to the last. Although proven wrong at all points of advancement in human history, this mentality still manages to flourish, and it saddens me. And don't forget—we create our reality.

Although we still haven't figured out the whole flying car thing. I guess we can't win them all. Here we are in the year 2021. I was told there would be flying cars…

Speaking of creating our realities, there was a thought experiment designed by physicist Eugene Wigner that is now famously known as Wigner's friend. It showed how two different people could experience two different realities simultaneously. Up until recently, it existed only as a thought experiment, a little mental conundrum to keep people from sleep. Last year, however, physicists noticed that our recent developments in quantum technology made it possible to actually conduct this thought experiment as an actual experiment. Massimiliano Proietti at Heriot-Watt University in Edinburgh and some of his buddies got together and actually created different realities and compared them. The results proved Wigner had been correct—two people can experience two different and irreconcilable realities, making it impossible to agree on objective facts. Looking at the political landscape in the USA today certainly makes one wonder if we haven't already proved this theory on a social scale. But of course, it's not as simple as that. Wigner's idea was of a polarized photon, which can have either a horizontal or vertical polarization. In his thought experiment, Wigner imagined a friend in a separate lab preparing to check the polarization of the photon. Before he checks it to see, the photon exists in the superposition of being in both polarized states at the same time (just like the Heisenberg principle or Schrodinger's cat). Wigner, meanwhile, in the same reality but in a different room, has no information about the results of his friend's test, so to him, the photon and the results of the test are in a superposition of all possible outcomes. The friend can even call and tell him that he has completed the experiment, but as long as he doesn't tell him the *results* of the experiment, Wigner's reality still exists with the superposition.

Now, to me, this just seems that they are overthinking common ignorance. Wigner is in a reality in which the results of the polarization test are unknown simply because his friend never told him the results of the test. What's so complicated about that? As in our society, people screaming about fake news are just not aware of the facts. But of course, physicists can't be satisfied with that. They need to know *why* the fake-news people are not aware of the facts and how this affects the very fabric of reality. So Proietti and Pals carried out an actual physical experiment using six entangled photons to create two alternate realities—one for Wigner and one for Wigner's friend. Wigner's friend confirms the polarization of the photon, and Wigner then performs an interference measurement to determine if the photon and its measurement are in a superposition (multiple possibilities). The result showed that both realities can coexist even with their differing outcomes. How does any of this make any sense? I have no idea. Let me tell you a quick story about me and physics.

When I was in grad school, I had to earn a math credit to graduate. I had been studying a lot about "UFOs" and propulsion systems (the aforementioned Robert Lazar was big news at the time), and so I had a keen interest in physics. I figured I might perform better in a math course that I had such a keen interest in. I was sorely mistaken. As it turns out, interest alone is of no use without the fundamental skills to understand the math. Three weeks into the course, my professor pulled me aside and said bluntly, "Matthew, you can't do this." I agreed. I had become keenly aware of my mathematical shortcomings. However, he was kind and understanding, and he said, "I have heard from your professors in the English department that you are a talented writer." (Yeah, let them read this drivel!) He continued, "If you write a five-page article each week on some new development in the world of physics and hand it in as your assignment, I will pass you for this class." And so that is exactly what I did. I got to read a lot of interesting articles, but as you can see from my rudimentary explanation of Wigner's friend, I struggled to grasp the larger implications. Still, the professor liked my papers and passed my math-incompetent ass.

My point here is that the physicists, the people who know far more about this sort of thing than I do, are all very excited as this experiment proves the power we have as observers of this reality, and it proves that our reality is not the concrete corporeal thing we thought it was. It is fluid, it is ethereal, and it is, as I have been trying to express in these ramblings, not what we thought. Our thinking is fundamentally flawed. Many brighter people than I believe this is because philosophy and science were separated back in Galileo's day. They are not separate studies but, in fact, are very much intertwined. Similar to my argument that magic and science are one and the same. Do we understand it or at least accept it as possible? Science. Is it crazy to even think about and impossible to accept? Magic. But give it a few years. You can wait while you sit in your car, streaming your favorite show on Netflix on your freakin' phone.

Anyway, what was I talking about? Ah yes, eternal life. Now as I have described earlier, eternal life is a given if you develop your soul integrity. Remember the bit about creating a mental sigil to link your memories and experiences and how to use it when you shuffle off this mortal coil to retain your identity? Well, science may well give you a leg up. Transhumanism is the idea of the next step in human evolution—combining our physical forms with our amazing new technology. I am a lazy ape, so I will cut to another journal entry for this bit. Enjoy!

Transhumanism: Making You Obsolete!

Transhumanism is the next step in human evolution, and it is already being taken. Humans are
merging and will continue to merge with technology. It is no longer science fiction but science
fact. In twenty to thirty years, humans will be a
very different species. What does this mean for
you, a lowly service-ape? The answer will disgust
you.

   This entry is an introduction to what I hope
will become a series of posts examining the physical, psychological, spiritual, ethical, and philo-
sophical implications of the impending jump
in human evolution known as *transhumanism*.
What is transhumanism, exactly? You can learn
all about it online. But if you are like me and
already have dozens of tabs open on your browser
and are loathe to open yet another, then read on.

   Let me begin with an example. Do you own
a toaster? The first commercial toaster was introduced by General Electric in 1909, model D-12.
Since then, toasters have become a countertop
staple in most American homes and, indeed,
European homes. You probably have a toaster sitting in your general vicinity right now. Now what
if you could surgically implant that toaster into
your torso? You could have toast anywhere, at any
time. With new advancements in nanotechnology, we could make a toaster that is 1/1000000
the size of your current toaster and inject it
directly into your stomach, where it could produce microscopic bits of toast. This *nano*-toaster
could produce toast on demand, and you could
make that demand just by thinking about how
good a bit of toast would be right now. Thus,

with the merging of our organic body with the technology of the toaster, the toaster-human hybrid is created. This is transhumanism.

Yes, that example is purely idiotic and just meant for fun. The actual possibilities go far beyond that, however. Technology evolves a lot faster than humans do. Just look at how much telephones have changed in the last forty years. They went from big plastic-encased clunky things that hung on the wall and couldn't even download pornography to a small handheld device that has more computing power than the computers NASA used to send the first men to the moon. In fact, they have more computing power than the most advanced computers of 1995. Scientists have a word for this: *doomsday*. No, wait, not that word. This one: *exponential* evolution. This means rather than following a standard progression of 1, 2, 3, 4, 5, 6…an exponential progression doubles, then triples, then quadruples, like this: 1, 2, 4, 8, 16, 32, 64…and on and on until you wake up one morning and you're an immortal being with superpowers. But we are getting ahead of ourselves. Let's look at the current state of transhumanism.

Scientists say that we are already technically cybernetic organisms, or "cyborgs," as so many of us walk around with our smartphones clutched in our pasty hands. Many modern people say that they could not function at full capacity in their day-to-day lives without this handheld augmentation. We use them to communicate, to access information, to watch videos, and to play little bowling games that distract us from the fact that the resulting field of microwaves we are living in is giving us all cancer. We have no need to worry, however, as transhumanism will soon equip us all with nanobots—tiny, microscopic robots—that will travel through our bloodstreams and destroy any cancer cells that develop before they become a nuisance. So fear not, proto-transhuman, your children will be fine! You, on the other hand, are already as good as dead. Although the technology is evolving faster and faster, it will still be a good twenty to thirty years before we are a go for nanobots (although "smart-pills" already have FDA approval).

Indeed, we as a species are on the precipice of a giant step forward in our own evolution, and this means taking control of our own evolution. As you know, anything that is made available to the public represents technologies as far as twenty years further on that already exist but are still in the research and development stage. What wonders does transhumanism hold? How about contact lenses that can take pictures or record video? So your partner won't let you record a sex tape? Well, then, tell them that twinkle in your eye is your undying love and not a livestream to your xxx website. (Note: This is a sad and outdated attempt at humor. If you do this, regardless of gender, you are an asshole.) Earbuds will be able to translate any language for you, just like Douglas Adams's Babel Fish.

RFID chips are already being used by soulless corporations like Google and, I want to say, DARPA (?). These radio-frequency identification chips are injected into the subcutaneous tissue just between the index finger and thumb and will open locked doors within the company headquarters (literally and figuratively). They will also serve as your payment in the company cafeteria, at vending machines, and allow you access to the company computer network. As we move into a cashless society (did I mention that? Because we are), these implants will allow you to buy food, water, and drugs with the swipe of your hand. In the very near future, food and water will be scarce, so you will definitely need an implant to survive. Nestlé sure as shit won't sell you any of their water without a chip, and they intend to own *all* the potable water (#BoycottNestlé).

I can already hear some of you religious types muttering "mark of the beast!" As it so sayeth in the Holy Book of Random Crap Collected Over Centuries and Heavily Edited and Mistranslated:

And he causeth all, both small and great, rich and poor, free and bond, to receive a mark in their right hand, or in their foreheads: And that no man might buy or sell, save he that had the mark, or the name of the beast, or the number of his name. (Revelations 13:6–7)

Well, rest assured, that is precisely what we are talking about. But transhumanism does not end there. Transhumanism can (and eventually will) bring about the merging of man and computer. Microchips can be hard-wired into the brain to give you the ability to instantly "learn" anything. Can't speak French? Chip! *Maintenant tu peux, toi magnifique bâtard!* Supposed to play Schumann's Toccata in C Major at the coffee house tonight but forgot to take piano lessons? Chip! You'll knock 'em dead! You want to learn how to calculate advanced physics but

145

can't afford the exorbitant price of tuition at an accredited university? Chip! I am only kidding about that last one, however. If you cannot afford tuition, you certainly won't be able to afford the chip. However, this raises the questions: (1) How can anyone be special if everyone is "special"? And (2) What of those that cannot afford these new enhancements? Will they be left behind to devolve? Will the human species split into two new species—the enhanced and the unenhanced? The simple answer: yes, we will. It's already happening.

Transhumanism represents a coming jump for the human species (well, some of us, anyway). From genetically modified "designer babies" and CRISPR technology that allows us to edit our very genomic code to added enhancements such as night or infrared vision, eidetic and photographic memory, and even Wi-Fi-like mind-to-mind telepathy, the human race is about to become...something else. Enhanced people will even be able to upload their "mind" into a computer, or better yet, an android that looks just like them. And it is going to happen a *lot* sooner than you may realize. Those contact lenses I mentioned should be on the market by 2025. By 2030, earbud translators and night vision. By 2040, mind-to-mind telepathy and Elon Musk's Neuro-Lace enhanced brain functions. As soon as 2050, we will have begun splitting into those two distinctive subspecies.

But what will become of the unenhanced? Will they be enslaved? Hunted for sport? Herded and used like pack animals? Taken by Morlocks into subterranean caves to be devoured at leisure? Who the hell cares? We certainly don't seem to

give a tin shit about the "lesser creatures" currently sharing our world. What's one more? And
mind you, I am well aware that I am on the path
of becoming one of the unfortunate unenhanced.

I am not joking about this. You will most
likely see exponential development in your lifetime. Young children have already adapted to a
world where things that cannot be downloaded,
clicked, or swiped seem unnatural. Unborn children will be born into a world where they will
already be enhanced—*if* they are in the right economic class. You see, the elite that are already dab-
bling in transhumanism, and who have already
fully accepted that this is the inevitable future of
the human species, are very concerned about population numbers. Not everyone will have a place
in this Brave New World, and they are already
culling the herd. This jump into evolutionary
hyperspace will leave many behind, but for those
that make the jump, transhumanism will take
them even further. From enhanced physical and
mental abilities too numerous to mention here to
virtually stopping the aging process.

Remember those nanobots? Imagine nanobots that will draw enough energy from your
body to run perpetually (just like a watch that
is powered solely by your heartbeat), have the
ability to replicate themselves, and their only
purpose is to travel around your body and repair
degrading cells. If you are thinking that immor-
tality could become a reality, you are on the right
track. And with an extended lifespan, the time
issue of interstellar travel is less of an issue.

Star Trek had it wrong. Unless Kirk or
Picard were cyborgs, then...oh, wait, the Borg.
No, they may have hit the nail on the head.

Transhumanism could—and most likely will—lead to a "hive mind" among the enhanced trans-humans. Right now, we are seeing the implementation of an "internet of things," where everything in your house can "talk" to other things in your house and you can boss them all around from your cell phone. Imagine what that concept would mean for an internet of the mind. You developed as a child by going through an educational system. It took you years to learn language skills, math skills, and any other skills you use to survive. Your children may have no need for that. Chip! Perhaps this is why our educational system is being allowed to shrivel up and die? They know it will be obsolete anyway.

This is happening. Make no mistake. Our future, and ourselves, will be unrecognizable. And it will happen in your lifetime.

This is not to say that transhumanism will be a good thing, of course—not with the way our society currently conducts itself. As the late, great Stephen Hawking put it in his final collection of essays, *Brief Answers to Big Questions*:

> We are now entering a new phase of what might be called self-designed evolution, in which we will be able to change and improve our DNA.... We have now mapped DNA, which means we have read 'the book of life,' so we can start writing corrections.

Although Dr. Hawking wisely suggests that this technology be confined to the repair of genetic defects, he also notes the threat it poses in our currently unbalanced civilization. He said that despite regulations that restrict this technology to the betterment of all humankind, there will be those "elites" who cannot resist the temptation and who will have the resources to broker for themselves greater intelligence, physical strength, sharper eyesight—hell, let's just call them what they are: superpowers. And if history has taught us anything about ourselves, it is that those who think themselves superior have a way of becoming aggressive and acting out. Hawking continues,

> Once such superhumans appear, there are going to be significant political problems with the unimproved humans, who won't be able to compete. Presumably, they will die out or become unimportant. Instead, there will be a race of self-designing beings who are improving themselves at an ever-increasing rate.

Superhuman rich people. What's not to love? Let's hope the Great Work can help turn the preternatural instincts of these people to feed the good wolf before they unleash this genetically modified bad wolf all over us, their poorer relations. Keep in mind, these "elites" are the same people whose past behavior has been so abysmal that it has sparked a conspiracy theory that they are, in fact, actually lizard people, or reptilians. And despite their best efforts to kill this idea, it seems to only have gained more traction in recent years. I would say that this notion stems from the idea that certain elements within the ranks of these elite act from the reptilian section of the human brain—the place from where ego, greed, self-preservation, and all the lower human impulses flow. The collective consciousness has picked up on this aspect of their nature and it has manifested in a collective image of "lizard people." We need to help these people to raise their own consciousnesses to the higher frequencies, help them to attain empathy, or we're all screwed. It's either that or take away all their money, and that would just be rude.

Where was I? Ah, yes, transhumanism. Remember the serpent in Genesis who told early humans they could "become like God"? You know how ever since religions have promised "eternal life"? These so-called gods had already merged with their own technology, and by creating us in their image, set us on the same evolutionary path. And now we will see it come to fruition. It is interesting how technological development seems to mirror spiritual development. Will the decision eventually be "natural or artificial"? The funny thing is, all this technology that led us to the artificial approach of transhumanism really started to develop back in 1947. The year 1947…why does that date sound familiar…? Ah, yes. 1947. Roswell.

CHAPTER 12

They Came from the Sky

So who started the human race down this path toward an eternal life as gods? Well, that depends on who you ask. If you have read the massive body of work produced by cuneiform scholar Zechariah Sitchin, then you probably know them as the Anunnaki. If you haven't read Sitchin's work (and you really should), the story—based on translations of the earliest stone tablets of human writing in cuneiform from Mesopotamia—goes that long ago, around one hundred thousand BC, an extraterrestrial explorer landed in the waters of the earth, hence becoming known as a bit of a fish-god since he (or she) had to come out of the waters. They found gold here. They wanted the gold to repair the atmosphere on their home world, which had depleted much as our own atmosphere here on earth has depleted, and yes, our scientists have since said that scattering gold dust particles in the upper atmosphere will help repair the damage and slow climate change. These Anunnaki colonized the earth and brought down their labor class to toil in mines to extract precious metals. The mines were unpleasant, and the workers revolted. And there was war in heaven. So this clever group of Anunnaki scientists, led by a fellow called Enki, came up with a plan to produce a hybrid slave race. As their geneticists were already conducting bizarre experiments with the local fauna (in which they produced a myriad of creatures that still exist in our collective memories as legends), they figured they could produce an adequate native worker. They then created modern humans by splicing some of their own DNA into the native australopithecines found rummaging for berries in the regions of the

Abzu, or Africa. Enki, incidentally, had set up laboratories in a region known for its snake population, and so his symbol among the new hybrid species was that of the serpent. This holds out today, as I mentioned earlier, in the form of the caduceus, the symbol of the American Medical Association.

Anyway, this is where the Old Testament comes from. It is a collection of these old stories from the earliest days of humanity. The wondrous things described in these books are merely early humans trying to describe technologies that were far beyond their understanding. This is why the book of Genesis says, "Let *us* make man in *our* image" and "They took wives from the daughters of man," and all that. Look it up. The working class of the Anunnaki, the Nephilim, were horny, I guess, or this is just representative of the crossbreeding program that utilized genetic splicing. Whichever you prefer, it's irrelevant. The point is that we are a hybrid species, whether by sex or science. This is why humans are so far advanced compared to the other animals that share our biome and roughly got the same start we did. Although—I should note—have you noticed that animals seem to have made a jump in cognition in recent years? I have. Dogs understand more language. Crows have become tool users. And ducks... I don't trust the ducks. They walk, they swim, they fly—they're a triple threat! But I digress. (By the way, the duck thing is just a running inside joke I have with myself. I am sure ducks are fine, honorable creatures. Still, I would love it if we could all start referring to a flock of ducks as a "conspiracy." Why not? A flock of crows is a "murder," and as I've said, they've become tool users. How creepy is that?)

To double back to what I mentioned earlier, this breeding program was apparently illegal, and there was more unrest in the heavens as other entities became involved in the debate as to what was to be done with us humans. It was decided to let us all get wiped out in the upcoming planetary shift—the one that caused our planet to tilt on its axis by precisely 23.5 degrees, thereby shifting the ring of sacred sites that marked our planet's former equator with structures built by these different visiting groups. The tilt would not only cause the massive shift of our electromagnetic field that would hide advanced outposts from our physical eyes, but it would also bring about the Great Deluge, the Flood of Noah. Enki and his team did not like the idea of seeing their creation wiped out. They saw promise in us. And while the "God" of Genesis—the entity in charge at the time who treated early humans as slaves—decided to leave the abomination that Enki had created to its fate, Enki took one trusted servant aside, a fellow by the name of Atra-hasis/Utnapishtim (aka Noah) and told him how to build a craft that could survive the flash flood. It wasn't really a big boat as depicted by most Sunday school stories. It was more of a gigantic, enclosed barrel (according to the dimensions laid out in Genesis 6:14–15). And Noah didn't herd all the animals of the world on board in pairs. He was most likely entrusted with DNA samples of animals native to the region (Mesopotamia) as well as live creatures. In case the big wooden barrel plan didn't pan out, Enki's people also relocated some early humans to what is now South America, where they would have a better chance of surviving the coming catastrophe. If you check your anthropology, you will see that around the time of the deluge, human civilization suddenly appeared in that part of the world, with similar tastes in architecture, agricultural skills, and stories of "serpent people from the sky."

All this is confirmable by your own hand if you are interested. Put your own mind to work, don't take my word for it. Could I be wrong? Of course. Only a fool thinks themselves infallible. But as I said, these Anunnaki were not the only species involved with humans, before or after the Deluge. By the way, I should note here that the Anunnaki were depicted as considerably larger than humans. Indeed, if you look at ancient carvings, you see very tall humanoids (with what appear to be knitted beards, I have no idea what that was all about. Go figure alien fashion) seated on thrones and holding court over tiny humans. As the book of Genesis says of the children of humans and the Nephilim, "there were giants in the earth in those days." Some say there still are giants around. We have certainly recorded the remains of enough of them. Interestingly, newspaper reports of discoveries of giant skeletons—some as large as thirty feet in height—were commonly reported in world media right up until the 1930s when suddenly the reports just stopped. Again, don't take

MATTHEW COLERIDGE

my word for it. Google it. Sadly, the so-called hidden history of our species, and any evidence thereof, has been spirited away to the basements of museums around the world. If you work in one of these museums, go find it and reveal it. It's time.

So to get back on track, there are several "races" of entities around us. Nordics, Tall Whites, Reptilians, Grays of various sizes, and that's just the tip of the iceberg. Government agencies refer to them as EBEs, or Extraterrestrial Biological Entities. More is being revealed every day, and disclosure is imminent. Some of these entities are malevolent, some benevolent, and everything in between, just as we humans are. By and large, they are benign. If they weren't, they could have wiped us all out eons ago.

If you have had any contact with them, then you know the ones that speak at any length tend to be kind, and they have a weird sense of humor that tends to rub off on those of us to whom they speak. I am reminded of one occasion reported by John Keel in his book *The Mothman Prophecies* when an alien ship was observed in the sky by several people. Just so that there was no mistake, the entities controlling it had taken the time to write the letters "UFO" on the hull of the craft. Now *that's* funny.

My own contacts, unlike the aforementioned fifth column Franklin, usually do not manifest physically but connect psychically. Often at night, I will have a weird dream and realize it is someone fucking with my head for fun. I wake up and feel the presence in the room with me, and we chat. Just so you know, these entities will usually not enter your home unless invited. It's a sort of protocol with them. I have a standing invitation with the stipulation that they are welcome to visit but only as a friend under the strictest definition of the word "friend." A little lighthearted trickery or joking is fine, but nothing that can have any ill effect on me or anyone else at all is permitted. My visitor(s) is usually the same entity, an entity that has always identified itself to me as "Elf." Elf first contacted me when I was in my early stages of this education I referred to earlier. This was when we lived in the new house after my father had died. At first, I had thought Elf was malevolent. ELF, I had been warned, stood for extremely low frequency, just like the ITU designation for electro-

154

magnetic radiation, radio waves with frequencies from three to thirty hertz. As it turned out, Elf was just using this designation as a way of identifying how they were communicating with me—me, being the one on the lower frequency. Elf also used the acronym TKEJ, which they told me back then meant "to know every joke," because as a child, I had collected joke books, loved comedy, and to this day have mad respect for stand-up comedians and writers of humor. Elf shared my love of humor, particularly absurdist humor, and that remains the basis of our friendship. I don't know why they like talking to me, but I am very happy that they do. I get the feeling it's always Elf or the same group of entities using that system. It is welcome to me, and I am often amazed at how I can happily sit at home, open a bottle of wine, smoke a little cannabis, what have you, and just have a chat with these entities. Of course, chemical enhancements are not necessary. We often chat without them, but for me, it's more fun as it helps my mind keep up with theirs. Either way, it always gets me laughing and makes me feel this overwhelming sensation of peace and love, and it raises my consciousness. I know that when I "die," shuffle off this meat-puppet, I will be in good company. But I also know that I will be back again, like a good Boddhisatva.

Incidentally, it was these Elf entities that told me I should start writing all this down to share with people. Like Enki before, they want information shared and proliferated, to the disapproval of the larger force of entities, who would prefer humans be kept out of the loop or oppressed, at least for now. These latter are the ones that make it hard for me to write about these things and try to prevent me from finishing this work, and this is why I just adopted Vonnegut's "swooping" method of writing. If I don't, I will never be able to share this. Again, I apologize for my dreadful writing, but it's the best I can do to get these thoughts out through the muddled interference. I invite you to contact me if you would like to talk about it in person. Perhaps I will be able to offer more clarity that way.

Speaking of dreadful writing, it occurs to me at this point to share a literary critique that I wrote a few years back. It's a review of Dan Brown's *Origin*. I will post it as an insert here because it carries information relevant to cattle mutilations and crop circles, topics I promised I would get to earlier. Before I share it, let me just say, I mean no disrespect to Dan Brown. I am a fan. And I am certainly no one to judge anyone else's writing style. My own style seems to be that I write the way Jackson Pollock painted (again, I know nothing about art). Dan Brown can at least organize a compelling story and paint a lovely, detailed picture of words. Respect. My issue with this novel is…well, just read it.

A Review of Dan Brown's *Origin*

Well, summer is upon us with its insufferable heat and cancer-causing UV radiation, so like many, I have taken it upon myself to hole up in a place devoid of sunlight to begin tapping into my summer reading list. First up this year: Dan Brown's *Origin*.

Let me begin by saying, yes, it is an enjoyable read. If you are not familiar with Dan Brown's work, he wrote the blockbuster *The Da Vinci Code*—the book that caused a big stir back in 2003 and got people discussing the possibility that Jesus was married. For the record, I think he was…but I also think his name was Yeshua, not Jesus. But that is a different topic. So is the fact that Brown has been sued before for plagiarism, most notably for *The Da Vinci Code*, which seems to have borrowed heavily from an academic work called *The Holy Blood and the Holy Grail* by Henry Lincoln, Michael Baigent, and Richard Leigh.

Before the wildly popular *Da Vinci Code*, Brown penned such other pop thrillers as *Deception Point* and *Angels and Demons*, and after it, he penned the pop thrillers *The Lost Symbol* and *Inferno*. While his novels are fun to read, they also have a tendency to be formulaic and predictable. If you know the plot of one, you know the plot of the rest: a huge earth-shattering religious/philosophical discovery is made, but someone will do anything to keep it secret—including murder. The murder is carried out by some ex-military type on the orders of a mysterious antagonist who is known only by a title, like "The Teacher" or "The Provost" or "The Regent." As the story progresses, the identity of this unknown villain is heavily hinted to be one person—but in a "surprising" twist, turns out to be someone quite close to the hero, Robert Langdon (except in the novels *Deception Point* and *Digital Fortress*, in which the protagonists are Rachel Sexton and Susan Fletcher, respectively). Langdon is an expert in code and symbology at Harvard University, but he spends most of his time traveling the world and bothering tour guides and tourists with his detailed answers to questions no one really asks.

One thing about Dan Brown's books, they certainly make you feel like your life sucks because you have never seen any of the amazing sights Langdon has. I imagine most of Dan Brown's loyal readers have a bucket list of travel destinations they know in their heart of hearts they will never start, let alone complete. Don't feel bad. I've been abroad for the past fifteen years and have traveled to twenty-five countries, and I have only seen three of the places he mentions in his traveloguesque tales, and a homicidal albino monk has not chased me through any of them. The plot of *Origin* follows the usual Dan Brown formula, but like I said, his books are still enjoyable. It's a fun read, the kind of book that sits atop the best-seller lists not because it is great literature but simply because it is fun. I dare say best-seller lists are a testimony to the mediocrity of the multitude of "average readers" that fancy themselves literati—those that pat themselves on the back for holding a novel rather than a cell phone, or even a Kindle. For these people, half the fun of reading a book is in having other people see them reading a book on the subway or in their local coffee shop (rather than some electronic gewgaw, which only stupid people use as entertainment). It gives them a needed sense of superiority. Yet whichever medium you choose to access your Dan Brown fix, you will still have fun reading it. And then when the movie comes out, you can annoy your friends by pointing out all the ways the script was lazy with its interpretation because lord knows all film adaptations of a book should be at least five hours long—you know, to really capture the detail of the novel. This is why, if you've never sat through the extended version of *The Lord of the Rings*, you've obviously missed the point entirely. I'm sorry, this is supposed to be a review of Brown's *Origin*, and yet I can't stop prattling on about everything else he has written. Well, I guess that is because, while despite my thinking that Brown's works are generally pop-lit and formulaic, I do still enjoy reading them. I buy them when they hit bookstores, I admit it. And yet while I enjoyed reading *Origin*, I was disappointed by it. Not because the identity of the "mysterious antagonist" was obvious from somewhere around chapter 6 (as I said, predictability has become the hallmark of a Dan Brown plot), but because the "big secret" of this particular story was a bit of a disappointment. It focuses on the age-old debate between science and religion: Is there a "God" or is life just a chemical reaction? And it always seems to come down to one or the other with no middle ground. Why can't it be both? And while the book does dabble in this possibility, the part of the book that stirred my ire can be found on pages 285–286 when the character of "NASA astrobiologist Dr. Griffin Bennett" is introduced by Brown for the sole purpose of killing any notions of the reader that this book might touch upon the extraterrestrial hypothesis. Dr. Bennett states in no muddled terms:

> When it comes to the notion of extraterrestrial life…there exists a blinding array of bad science, conspiracy theory, and outright fantasy. For the record, let me say this: Crop circles are a hoax. Alien autopsy videos are trick photography. No cow has ever been mutilated by an alien. The Roswell saucer was a government weather balloon called Project Mogul. The Great Pyramids were built by Egyptians without alien technology. And most importantly, every extraterrestrial abduction story ever reported is a flat-out lie.

For the record, let me say this: this "Bennett" is a poor scientist. He obviously has done no serious investigation of these points before simply regurgitating the accepted and acceptable mainstream school of thought on these topics. Just for the record, all crop circles are not made by two drunken clods with a board and some rope. Not the *real* ones. Look into it. The "circles" are complex and encoded with precise geometrical data, and the stalks of the plants that are flattened to form them are *unbroken* and altered on a cellular level. These unique traits are impossible to reproduce with the heavily pushed "drunk farmers with a board" method. Don't take my word for it, look it up.

As for the Roswell "saucer" being from Project Mogul, the short answer is this: the Roswell incident occurred in July 1947. Project Mogul was a program to detect radioactive particles in the atmosphere from Russian nuclear tests. Mogul did not begin until the early 1950s as the Soviet Union did not test nuclear weapons before 1949. When people checked the Mogul theory and found the dates to be off, the official story changed to say that Mogul began in 1947. Why, when the USSR did not have nukes to test until 1949? I don't know what may have crashed at Roswell, other than it was a UFO—that is, it is still technically *unidentified*, which is all a UFO is.

And cattle mutilations are certainly not just caused by natural predators or "satanists." Look at the surgical cuts, the cauterized wounds, and the complete exsanguination of the animal with no vascular collapse and no blood spatter or footprints around the carcass. Something doesn't add up, but no one takes time to really investigate or to listen to those that have as they get shouted down by the so-called skeptics. I'm a skeptic too—and I am skeptical of the "official" explanation.

Finally, saying that all reports of alien abductions are flat-out lies is incredibly insensitive to the obviously legitimately traumatized people who believe they have experienced them, and as far as the Great Pyramid at Giza, really? Ancient Egyptians built that? Then *do it again*. Even with our modern technology, you can't. Someone should. No matter how much it would cost, it would certainly be worth it to get "conspiracy theorists" like me to shut the fuck up once and for all.

It's easy to accept the official stories simply because they are "official"—but come on. Do you really think the government and media never lie to you? People need to do more research into these topics before they believe whatever they are told. *That* is "bad science." As the book itself argues, if we are not open to new ideas and questioning the "official" answers, we end up killing the ideas of people like Galileo, Copernicus, and Darwin (and often killing the people themselves). If we always accepted the "official" story over true investigation, we would still think the earth is flat and be afraid of sailing off the edge. In this regard, Dan Brown and others like him shoot their own arguments in the balls (if their arguments *had* any balls to shoot).

Man, I suck at book reviews! And this is because I, too, have an agenda. Let's get back to the book to get to that agenda, shall we? The title is, of course, *Origin*, and it gets this title from the search for the origin of life on earth. The book promises to offer an answer to the age-old questions, *Where do we come from? Where are we going?*—and it repeats and repeats and repeats these two questions to the point of annoying the holy hell out of this reader. And yes, this book does a very good job at attempting to answer these questions in a thrilling and suspenseful way, but it focuses mainly on the simplistic and binary populist argument: (a) God did it or (b) random natural chemical reactions did it.

Can't it be both? A little from column A and a little from column B? And when I suggest that perhaps there was a God-figure spiking the primordial soup, I mean the scientific possibility of the extraterrestrial hypothesis. Where do we tinfoil hat types get this crazy idea? From the very texts that are responsible for the idea of creationism—the same source that gave us the apparently all-too-believable "magic and invisible skyman" idea. How is that acceptable and the idea of an advanced alien species is not? Where's the logic?

The ancient Sumerian tablets that gave us our religious texts, the very same source of the creationist theory, when looked at in the literal sense rather than the fantastical, actually do tell a story that hints *very* heavily at the ET hypothesis. The original language of these texts has been mistranslated and edited by countless scholars and kings for over two thousand years now, and yet we can still see indicators of possible extraterrestrial handiwork in our collective origin stories. Countless works have been written on the topic, and all of them examine the original cuneiform tablets, the original languages, the etymologies, and yes, even the scientific possibilities—scientific possibilities that our current civilization has just begun to understand for ourselves in the last fifty years, such as space travel, genetic modification, and cloning. Of course, when our ancestors wrote of them more than five thousand years ago, they seemed like magic. If you went back in time to 7000 BC with an iPad, you might be written into the ancient texts as a "god" yourself.

The word used for "god" was "Elohim"—a *plural* noun, meaning "great ones." If you and your family were sitting in your own filth in a cave without so much as a piece of flint in your technological arsenal and, all of a sudden, some dudes floated down from the sky in a shiny metallic spaceship and showed you a YouTube tutorial about how to forge bronze tools, you just might think of them as "great ones" yourself.

Is it really so unacceptable to look at these ancient writings and think that maybe, just maybe, there was some life-changing extraterrestrial interplay? Wouldn't that be important enough to inspire the creation (or introduction) of the first written language known to humanity, just to record such a historical occasion?

The evidence is there if you just look for it, and I dare say there is more evidence for the ET hypothesis than there is for the "magic man in the sky" hypothesis. Ancient religions will not tell you about it because it's bad for their business. And new religions like science and government will not tell you about it because it is also bad for *their* business. I mean, who is going to change all those museum exhibits to include all the weird stuff archaeologists have been digging up for the past hundred years?

Is religion a bad thing? Not necessarily. It gives idiots with inherent violent tendencies a reason to behave themselves. Is science a bad thing? Not necessarily. It gives us medicine and a better knowledge of ourselves and our world. But they are both double-edged swords as they both can represent tremendous sources of power, and the one truth about human nature is that *power corrupts.*

Origin is a fun read. I enjoyed it. However, its simplification of a very complex issue pissed me off. Never let anyone tell you that that's all there is. There is very strong evidence to suggest that there is more—quite a bit more, in fact—to the story of our origins. While I encourage you to read, I encourage you to read everything you can. Don't just read what the mainstream tells you to read. Don't believe them when they tell you that's all that there is and to suggest otherwise is "bad science." That's what they tried to tell Copernicus. And now we look back on those who held authority over him as cruel and small-minded zealots.

Everyone has an agenda, even me. Get all the information. Do your own research. I know it is time-consuming, but the alternative—believing those in power, accepting without question what the current authorities tell you is truth...yeah, that's never caused any problems before, right?

While I did enjoy the book, I obviously do not entirely agree with its conclusions. I, personally, do believe that humans have had their genetic chemistry spiked by someone else, and I believe that the evidence of this is all around us, but there have been some very powerful interests involved in keeping it secret. Remember at the top of this post, I said that I am hiding away from the cancer-causing UV radiation of the summer sun? Why do you think it is that no other species on earth seems to have trouble with the local environment (that is until we come along and fuck it up)? Why do you think it is that, despite the idea that all life on earth was created by the same spark of chemistry, only humans have developed to the level that we have? Why do we need to change the food sources here before we can consume them? We cook our meat, and we have been genetically modifying the local vegetation to make it palatable to us since the beginning of human history when we developed agriculture seemingly out of the blue (oddly enough, right around the same time that these "gods" were allegedly poking their advanced noses into our primitive progress). No other species does these things. And of all the species on this planet, we're the only ones that, if left outside without proper supplies, will die of exposure.

I do agree with the answer *Origin* supports for the second question, *Where are we going?* This is the idea that humans are about to merge with the technologies we are creating. Tech is evolving exponentially, much faster than we are. It could even lead to "eternal life" through cancer-killing nanotechnology and cellular regeneration—the very "eternal life" that all religions seem to have been promising from day one and have yet never really been able to deliver. Perhaps this is what our "gods" were talking about thousands of years ago when they first showed up?

I am aware that these ancient "great ones" are still watching us. Perhaps they have us quarantined because their genetic experimentation has taken a wrong turn, we are still very primitive and dangerous, or perhaps they are more involved in our lives than we are aware. Either way, I, for one, am certain that there is truth in both ideas: life can begin naturally, but "god[s]" can accelerate it and guide it to a lasting experience as long as everyone remembers the golden rule: Be nice. Don't kill. And keep learning. There is no place for zealotry in religion or science. Nor is there any place for burying evidence that doesn't fit the promoted and accepted "official" version of any story. All evidence must be examined and considered, no matter how unsettling it may be. Otherwise, what good is a devotion to truth? Science becomes another religion, and we die in dogma rather than achieving our full potential. *Origin* by Dan Brown is available now! So is a lot of other interesting stuff with a bit more of an informative approach. Get to your local bookstores and libraries now before the evil summer sun gives you cancer.

CHAPTER 13

Travel Light, Travel Smart, Travel Safe

Well, I guess this mess of words contains everything I wanted to share with you in some random place or another. As I said, feel free to jump around. Take what you find useful. I am just happy I have managed to get it all (most of it, anyway) out of my head. I hope it takes some of the existential dread out of the life equation. A quick final point: Don't make regeneration your goal in your meditations. Let it be a byproduct of the pursuit of your own true purpose, which is identifying your true self, a soul within a vessel, and your role among the universal consciousness. Focus on that integrity. Also, never give things for free to people who you know can afford them. Give freely to those you know who cannot afford. Just a random thought there.

I do want to include a couple of travel tales here at the end of this rambling collection of thoughts. After all, I have spent the last fifteen years of my life traveling around the world, and I have had some experiences you may find interesting. Western culture tends to poopoo and mock tales of the invisible realm, but other cultures take it very seriously. Let me tell you about my personal experiences with two of them.

The first is a tale of castles, canyons, and cursed tablets, and it comes from the time I spent teaching in the Sultanate of Oman. Oman is a lovely country, known as the Switzerland of the Middle East because they don't get caught up in that whole Sunni-Shi'ite dispute. They love everybody (with the possible exception of the

Yemeni), and they all pray together. Seriously, the Omanis are some of the kindest people I have met. Their country is incredibly hot, however. In my first week there, I actually had a pair of shoes melt right off my feet. Some of the new professors and I were walking back to our apartment building from campus as the semester hadn't officially started yet, and so there was no shuttle service running. There are taxis, but on this day, they were few. So we started to walk the roughly two kilometers back. As we walked, I noticed my shoes had started making a crunching sound. The rubber had melted off the soles, and the plastic frames underneath were cracking as I walked. Soon, the soles of my feet had replaced the soles of the shoes. I had brought them with me from Korea, so I guess they just weren't made for the Arabian heat.

It was so terribly hot there, and the Omanis so kind, that if they saw you walking on the side of the road, even if they were heading in the other direction, they would turn around and offer you a ride. Oman is a very progressive country as well, and the girls are allowed to attend university right alongside the boys. They must sit on the opposite side of the classroom and no contact is permitted between the two genders, but they are allowed to attend. And the girl students were eager to learn. They volunteered to read, they volunteered to answer questions, and they volunteered to step up and write sentences on the board. They had something to prove, you see. The boys could not be bothered. It was like teaching two different classes simultaneously. One thing that would get all the students talking, however, was asking them to explain Islamic culture to me. And I was eager to learn.

One day, I told my students that I had plans to visit the famous souq (markets) in Nizwa. We lived in al-Rustaq, and Nizwa was another town about a two-hour drive away. My students said, "Oh, teacher, be careful! Do not go to the Nizwa souq after dark! There is black magic there!" They were serious. Arabic culture still speaks of the Djinn and black magic, entities, and powers from beyond the Veil. And yes, they take it seriously, as they should. My first semester at al-Rustaq was the autumn semester, and in November, the birthday of His Majesty Sultan bin-Said Qaboos (blessings be upon his name!) is celebrated. The four-day weekend holiday just happened to coincide with Thanksgiving in the US, and so some friends and I—one other American, a guy from New Zealand, and two ladies from Romania (both of whom I had worked with during my first year in Korea! Talk about a small world. Expat paths cross often)—decided to go camping near Nizwa. Our plan was to take two Jeeps—well, one Jeep and a Kia Sportage—and drive out through the wadis and camp at Jibreen Castle. Then we would drive up to Jebel Shams, the Grand Canyon of Oman, to check out some of the country's natural splendor.

As we drove through the wadis, we had to stop frequently to remove rocks from our path. At one point, two goat herders came down from the hillside and helped us lift heavy stones. They asked where we were traveling (even the rural folk in Oman speak pretty good English, as Oman had once been a British protectorate). We told them, and they warned us that the winter floods from the previous year had washed out many of the goat path roads we would be needing to traverse. It rains maybe twice a year in Oman, during the winter months. It doesn't happen often, but when it does, watch out. The ground is baked solid, so the wadis quickly flood, and roads are washed out. Every year, people are killed by flash floods. During my time in Oman, our university lost four students—one to a car accident (the leading cause of death in Oman), one to a heart defect (despite Oman having excellent health care), and two students who drowned in the wadis. The goat herders said our route was likely impassable, but we decided to try our luck anyway.

At one point, we found ourselves stopped below a rise in the road, where a landslide had covered our only means of progress. We got out of our vehicles and began moving rocks once again. One of the rocks I picked up was perfectly rectangular, about an inch thick, and it appeared to have deep scratches on one side, as though someone had used it to sharpen a knife. It struck me as so odd that I showed it to my companions. They agreed it was odd and continued to move rocks. Not one to shirk my end of the labor, I tossed the flat stone down into the wadi and resumed assisting with the rock removal. Soon we were on our way again, but not three minutes into our drive, I broke out in a bumpy rash. I became feverish, nauseous, and achy. Soon I had traded my shotgun seat with my Kiwi friend so that I could lie down in the back seat. I was trembling and obviously very sick. My friends became worried. As we drove, I listened to them discussing what we should do. The road we were on continued through the desert for another hour before it came to a T-intersection. At the intersection, we could go left to our planned destination or go right to a hospital. If we went to the hospital, it was another hour-long drive, so the camping trip would have to be canceled. All we could do was continue our drive and see how I felt by the time we reached the T. The bouncing of the Jeep on that desert road was killing me, and I began to wonder if I was going to die. About thirty minutes later, my stomach started to convulse, and I felt...let's just call it an irresistible urge. My friend slammed on the breaks, and I opened my door and crawled out of the Jeep. They rushed over to try to help me, and I crawled along the doors to the front of the Jeep, and I said to my friends, "Do not watch this!" and to my Kiwi friend, I said, "Run back up the road. If the girls catch up, stop them! They do not need to see this!" And leaning up against the front of the Jeep, I dropped trousers and just let it go. My body was purging horrible liquid from both ends. When I finally finished, my fellow American handed me a roll of paper towels to clean myself up with. We called to our Kiwi pal, who had stopped the girls just as they were about to catch up to us. I assume they figured out what was happening, but I still tried my best to kick dirt over the pile of foulness I had just purged upon the earth. My friends double-checked that I was okay. I told them I felt worlds better. My fever had broken, my rash was gone, and I had stopped trembling. I was, however, feeling very dehydrated. They handed me one of our bottles of water, and I crawled back into the Jeep and we were on our way once more. We reached the T soon after, and they said, "Well, Matt, what do you think? Will you live?" I would. We turned left and had dinner at the first restaurant we saw. The rest of the trip was amazing. I highly recommend a trip to Oman to see just how beautiful the mountains of Jebel Shams are.

To this day, however, I still wonder about that flat stone with the scratches on one side. Could the scratches possibly have been

Arabic? I lived in Oman for nearly two years, and I still have no idea how to read Arabic. Hangul (Korean) is a much easier language to read. A few years after this incident, I read an article about Roman curse tablets. Could I have found one of these, an old cursed clay tablet that had been buried until the floods had washed that section of hillside into the road? My Omani friends tell me that this, in their opinion, was most likely the cause of my sudden bought of illness.

My second tale of encounters with cultures that retain a deep connection to the old beliefs comes from an incident with which I began this book: my heart trouble on Halloween in Seoul. As I was making my way out to meet my friends that night, I started feeling very poorly on the subway platform waiting for the train to take me from Seoul Station to Noksapyeong. I felt so poorly, in fact, that I had to sit on one of the benches and rest and just let the train go by because I did not feel like moving. As I sat there, a gentleman that had gotten off the train strolled by. He wore a long black coat, black hat, and carried a black briefcase. He noticed me sitting on the bench, and he came over and sat right by me. There were other benches. And there was even room on my bench. But he sat directly beside me, his back to me but nearly touching me. As I swayed a bit, I lightly bumped him a few times. Still, he sat there. I got a very bad feeling about this man. At first, I was afraid he had noticed I did not look well and that he was going to try to speak to me, to ask if I needed help. He didn't. He just sat there, back to me, and just made me feel worse. I started to get angry. When the next train came by, I struggled to my feet and jumped on, despite the fact that I was now feeling much worse than when I had first sat down. I just wanted to get away from that asshole. My whole mind was scream-ing, *Fuck that guy! Why couldn't he just go away?* By the time the train got to Noksapyeong, I was starting to feel a little better but still not top-notch. You can flip back to the introduction of this book for a refresher on how that turned out. Short answer: three-day stay in the cardio ICU at Severance Hospital.

The following Tuesday, I was back on campus, feeling fine, and ready to teach my classes. However, when I went to my first class, I saw a note on the door, written in Hangul, that said, "Professor

Matthew's classes are canceled this week due to illness." (See, I told you Hangul was easier to read than Arabic. At least, it is for me.) I went to the office to make sure they didn't need me. As I sat waiting for the office admin staff to get back from lunch, one of my coworkers came into the office. He is from Romania. He and I hadn't talked much before this day, but he came over anyway to see how I was feeling. A very kind gesture. I told him my story, about the nagging ache in my sternum, how I ended up in the hospital, and for some reason, even the annoying guy that had sat next to me in the subway. His expression grew very serious, and he lifted his head to me and said, "I don't know how you will take this, Matthew. I know Americans find this sort of belief foolish, but I tell you that was no man." He went on to tell me that being from Romania, he had been brought up in a culture that truly takes the concept of vampires seriously. He said, "They are not like in the movies, drinking the blood and all that. Some do, but that's not really their power. They drain you of life energy." He said this man, this entity, that had spotted me on the subway had spotted an easy meal. He said he had sat so close to me to feed on my suffering. And I recalled, I did feel worse after he sat by me and a little better after I had left him. He nodded and said, "I have seen such creatures on the Seoul subway. It is a bad place for these beings." He warned me that if I ever feel sick that I should avoid crowds, as these entities will be drawn to the sick. He said, "Even animals when they are sick, they try to isolate to protect themselves. Get to a corner, get away from everyone, until you feel well enough to move again." Incidentally, it was this fellow who gave me the analogy of different worlds being like the sea—the further down you go, away from the light, the uglier the creatures get. And to hear him tell me all this with his Romanian accent really added that authentic touch. He and I started meeting for coffee on a regular basis after that, and he told me a lot about the Romanian culture and their understanding of the dark side of these entities. He also told me that it is not good to die in a hospital, that "those places are vortices of death, and it is easy for a soul to get lost." This is why I believe a sigil is useful. He said, "Recall what Master Nietzsche said, the best death is found in battle or in bed surrounded by loved ones." For me, the best death would be to die in my sleep, having one of those weird dreams that turn out to be an Elf playing a friendly trick on me. Then I will know I am among friends. But whatever. As I said, no matter how you go, go with a smile.

Incidentally, when I do die, this husk I leave behind is nothing but that—an empty shell. Still, I would hope that it not be mutilated, pumped full of unnatural chemicals, and sealed up in an aluminum box. I think the best thing for a body is to cremate it, bury it *au natural*, or just leave it in the wilderness and let nature do what nature does, as the Tibetan monks used to do. Donate organs to those in need, surely, but no chemicals. Why do we do that to our dead?

Whatever you may think about the extraterrestrial/ultraterrestrial presence, or otherworldly entities, you're going to have to incorporate it into your reality eventually, in some form or another. Following the news these days, we are starting to see a more open discussion of it from the top. The US Navy has released videos and admitted that these unknown objects are real (and they aren't always just spaceships), intelligence agencies are releasing once-classified documents, and more reliable sources are stepping forward with information, including Canada's former Minister of Defense, who testified that there are at least four different groups of entities interacting with us today. Names like J-Rod, the Grinning Man, and Skinny Bob are becoming more common in discussions of these topics. From my own experience, the Nordics are very enlightened, the Reptilians are a bit standoffish as they do not care for humans at all, the Tall Grays are all science and a bit sinister, and the Short Grays are more like biological/artificial androids than self-realized independent entities. In fact, a lot of these "craft" that we are seeing today do not carry the physical form of their pilots but only their *consciousness*, their mind/soul. The craft themselves are living, programmable organisms. This opens up a lot of possibilities in regard to interstellar travel. Imagine if you could put just your mind into a programmable bio-suitcase and not have to worry about such things as g-forces or radiation. Our species is already figuring out how to create programmable DNA. In fact, just recently a team of researchers created the world's first *xenobot*, which is described as "neither a traditional robot nor a known species of animal. [It is] a new class of artifact: a living, programmable organism." This is essentially what the short Gray EBEs are. Despite being very advanced biosynthetic androids, they have distinctively feminine characteristics, and in some situations, they project a very comforting energy. They'll sit very close to you, try to hold your hand—it's kind of cute. Perhaps this is why they are used in so many abductions. Remember, not all these entities or EBEs or UTs are bad. Some are really kind, and really cool. Just remember, never let them approach unless they agree to approach in a genuine spirit of friendship. That's binding. Never invite them into your home unless they are bound as friends. But certainly, make friends where you can.

Remember Plato's *Allegory of the Cave*, how it represents our limited view of reality quite well in that we are indeed all just watching shadows on the walls of our skulls. The *real* world exists beyond our physical perceptions, and it is so much more. There are many powerful people in this world that would prevent you from ever knowing this. I am lazy, so I just have a simile of the cave. Trying to express all these odd thoughts that have been shared with me over the course of my existence is like having a massive collection of artifacts inside a cave with a very tiny opening as the only access. You want to bring everything out and share it with everyone, but only a little bit can be carried out at a time, and it is very time-consuming, and my limited brain can't handle the workload or solve the puzzle of how to extract everything in an orderly manner. The ramblings here represent that extraction effort. I have been aware of the frequencies and the wholeness of the real world, and of the Great Work, over the course of more than one lifetime. For some reason, it is in this lifetime that I am motivated to share it regardless of the risk of making a fool of myself. I feel I have to. It is my *raison d'être*. And besides, as I explained to friends who asked why I am writing this book, making a fool of myself is kind of my thing. It's very on-brand for me.

While Plato's cave represents the limited illusion that is our perceived reality, my cave represents the ideas that are occult and difficult to share. Also, my cave has dinosaurs. Troodons, to be specific. Stenonynchosaurs, to be even more specific. Did you know there is evidence that they were tool users? They had a rotatable third claw that could be used as an opposable thumb. Such potential. Imagine if their tool-making brains had allowed them to survive the extinction-level event that killed off the majority of their kind? They would have had millions of years of evolution and development on us. Curious, that.

ADDENDUM

In closing, let me just say thank you for your time. I hope you found something useful, or at least entertaining, in this rambling mess of a warning flare message. I know these topics are not for everyone, but they are real. I guess these ideas just make some people uncomfortable, and that's all right. The universe is nothing if not patient. Take all the time you need, but eventually, you will be assimilated. See, that's me trying to be funny again. I made several weak attempts in this book to be funny. I hope you noticed a few of them, and maybe even laughed at one or two. Remember the Two Rules for life and do your best to live by them. I truly believe it will make this world a better place and help slow, if not stop, our descent into the lower realms. And don't forget, when your time does come, greet death with love, joy, and laughter. And prepare your sigil. Again, I apologize for my random and disorganized writing style. It really was difficult to blurt all this out, and it is difficult to think through the white-noise fog that seems to fill my head whenever I try to communicate things of this nature. I did my best.

A final thought regarding simulation theory: when discussing these topics with people, I am often asked if I believe that we exist in some sort of simulated or artificial universe. The short answer is yes. However, it is not any simulation that we can fully understand just yet. The concept is new to us, as we have only begun creating our own versions of artificial environments and simulations within our computers. The system that creates our reality is beyond our current comprehension. We are seeing the apple and have no concept of the orchard or the planet on which it grows, nor the universe in which that planet exists. The ideas and technologies we can understand within our conscious minds must fit into the preexisting criteria of our understanding. In short, to comprehend it, we first have to be able to *see* it, and to see it, we must be capable of comprehending it. This reflects back to the notion of "negative hallucination," which I touched upon at the end of chapter 6. Any simulation this reality may, in fact, be is likely preparing us to take on real-world, or "base reality" roles, but we will not be allowed into that "real" world until we can show that we have perfected traits like compassion and empathy. This is why the Two Rules are so important. If we look at simulated game play (video games) in our world, we are aware that there are plenty of people who play these games for the destructive aspect, and they hurt or kill as many people as possible because, why not? These avatars and NPCs (nonplayer characters) are not real, so there is no real consequence for it. Yet to these higher consciousnesses observing the game play, what does this tell them about the individuals who are capable of seeing others as inconsequential or disposable? In our video games, it may not matter, but in our reality, it certainly does, whether it is simulated or not. Evidence and arguments supporting simulation theory are growing as we develop. Extraterrestrials may also be simulated characters, controlled avatars of players from someplace else who have hacked into our system. Ultraterrestrials might be maintenance personnel who come in from time to time to iron out any glitches in the matrix. The catacombs that are said to exist beneath Giza, underground cities like the one found in Derinkuyu, the Cappadocia region of Turkey, even the tales of Agartha and Hollow Earth Theory remind me of the underground maintenance tunnels beneath "simulations" like Walt Disney World. There's a lot that goes on behind the scenes to keep the illusion running smoothly. Perhaps EBEs are General Adversarial Networks, and they are from a competing AI system. They want to learn to replicate us to better infiltrate our system, and perhaps this already happened long ago. Perhaps they do it to act as benevolent guides, to keep us on the path of our proper spiritual evolution, and to promote the completion of the Great Work. Still, we are meant to evolve, overcome, and grow so that we can move on to these higher frequencies, or other realities, and who knows? The world outside this one could also be a simulation operating in another simulation inside another simulation… Turtles all the way down. Perhaps there is no "base reality" anymore, if there ever was. This may be a fractal of multiverses, each creating the others. As I said, we may be a "God" outside of time creating itself.

People also ask me what I think of the Mandala effect. I think people have flawed memories. Lord knows *I* do. Nonetheless, realities flow like water and can converge or diverge on their way to the sea. As we move forward with these concepts and our awareness develops, I think our reality is becoming much larger. We are crossing a certain milestone in the evolution of our collective consciousness. Something is about to change, and how that change manifests is up to us, as a collective. We can program the system from within, as indicated by the Princeton EGG Global Consciousness Project and the uncertainty principle.

Finally, I am sure I will recall things I left out just as sure as new ideas will occur to me as I progress toward the end of this incarnation. I will share them when they occur to me. In the meantime, if you would like to read more of my struggle to express ideas beyond my ability, I have a blog. You knew this was coming, didn't you? "Read my blog!" Really, it's not great, or even good by any means, but like this book, you might find something interesting in that mess. It's not for everybody, but if you connect with it, then you know it's for you. It's all for you. The blog is www.thecontemplativeape.com, and it is meant to be funny and entertaining, and hopefully a spark for enlightenment on something you will find useful. You will find what you need, whether I put it there intentionally or not, or whether it comes from me or not. In the end, the only thing that I can attest to with full commitment is this: *I don't know.* I am just trying to share with you what has been shared with me. Is every point in this book accurate and true? No. It is only as I understand it to be. For you, from your perception, it may be different. The larger truth of this is very real, and it is so for all of us. But when you start to break it all down into the finer points, there is entropy. When you get down into the quantum realms of any reality, things fall apart, and in that outside real-world realm, beyond time, beyond these corporeal shells, there is also a sense of progression, but rather than things falling apart, they come together. Recall that famous quote from Friedrich Nietzsche, "From chaos comes order." That is an incomplete thought. It's half of the cycle. From chaos comes order, and from order comes chaos, and 'round and 'round it goes. I don't think Nietzsche was the sort to use the phrase "'round and 'round," though. He seems like a fairly severe individual.

It's a bit like trying to assemble a puzzle from a pile containing pieces of thousands of different puzzles. Referring again to my personal allegory of the cave, this book is sort of a smash-and-grab job. I hope that in my hurried efforts, I have given you something useful, or at least entertaining, within its contents. Either way, may this whirlwind of information help bring us all together at some point, raise us to the higher frequencies of heaven, and enable us to complete the Great Work so that we can all—*all* of us—create a world in which all our dreams become reality.

Be nice.

Seek truth.

Build integrity.

Excerpt from The Spaces Between

"You ever been to Montana?" Stan was asking Aaron. Aaron was falling asleep in the window seat of the airplane that Stan had booked for them not twelve hours ago. From the moment that he had agreed to go on this little sojourn into the upper Midwest, Aaron's head had been spinning.

He had cured his hangover by having a few cocktails at the Lone Nut offices while Stan and Kite had made their travel arrangements. Since then, he had maintained a steady heavy buzz. Stan had realized that there would be a lot of driving involved, and neither he nor Aaron was a good candidate for that part of their journey, so he had invited another photographer along to act as a driver. The photographer's name was Martin something, but Stan just kept referring to him as "Scoop," taking what he probably thought was a secret delight in the way that nickname annoyed the young man. Now all three of them were wedged into those tiny little economy airplane seats, somewhere in the skies between Pittsburgh and Great Falls, Montana. Aaron was drifting off again, so Stan turned his banter on young Martin, who occupied the unfortunate middle seat between them.

"How 'bout you, Scoop? You ever been to Montana?"

"Not yet," the photographer replied.

"Beautiful up there," Stan informed him in his best Indian Chief voice. "Big Sky country! Elk and…whatnot." He took another sip of his gin and tonic and rang for the flight attendant.

"Hel-lo… Janet," he said, reading her nametag and handing her a business card. "I'm with *Lone Nut* magazine. Would you ask the pilots if they have any UFO sightings they'd like to report? Professional pilots are always good witnesses, even if they are drunk."

Janet smiled, and a small, fake-polite laugh escaped her. "I don't know, sir. I'll ask," she said, taking the card. Stan watched her walk down the aisle.

"See that, Scoop? You never know where you might find a good story."

"Marty," replied the photographer.

"What?"

"My name's Marty."

"Sure thing," Stan continued. "You're gonna love Montana, Scoop. Did you remember to bring film?"

"Of course."

"Good. Some people might forget, but not you, Scoop."

"Why do you insist on calling me Scoop?"

Stan studied Marty for a moment. "So you're a traditionalist?"

"What?"

"You're a traditionalist," Stan said, gesturing to Marty's camera with his drink. "You still use film."

Marty smiled. "Yeah, I like film. Digital, anybody can screw with it. Film is more truthful."

"Good. In this line of work, we need all the truth we can get."

"Really?" Marty turned to face Stan for the first time on this flight. "I get the opposite impression. Seems to me, you need all the hype you can get."

Stan was caught off guard, but he shrugged it off. "Well…hype, truth…can't they be the same thing once in a while?" Marty just shook his head, and Stan took that as a teaching opportunity. "Have you heard of the Mystery Airships of the 1890s?" he asked.

"Of course," Marty replied. "Anyone who has studied UFO folklore has read something about them."

"Excellent. You've done some research. What can you tell me about them?"

Martin thought for a moment. "Well, if I remember correctly, there was a rash of sightings around North America in the 1890s, most famously in the San Francisco area, of what were described as long dirigible-like crafts that were occupied by a bunch of partiers dressed in the current fashions."

"Okay," Stan pushed him. "And what were they doing?"

Martin shrugged. "Nothing, really. Just flying around, scaring locals and making headlines in little Podunk newspapers."

Stan winced. "No, Marty. No newspaper is 'Podunk.' The printed word is power. A free press is essential to a free democracy. And that is a big part of what has happened to the US. Our noncorporate press is ignored and overshadowed by the big corporate propaganda news agencies. Never call any newspaper 'Podunk.' They are free." Stan took another sip of his G&T. "So. What did these Podunk papers say about the airships?"

Martin found himself a little touched by Stan's passion for the free press. He started to take the conversation a little more seriously. "I really don't recall. One allegedly landed in a farmer's field and asked the farmer and his son for some water. When the farmer asked them where they were from, they said they were from Mars."

"Precisely!" Stan said, spilling a little of his drink on Martin's knee. "So what do you make of that?"

Martin shook his head. "What's to make of it? They obviously weren't really from Mars."

"How do you know that?" Stan said.

Martin looked incredulous. "It was an airship, a balloon... Technology like that from the 1890s simply wasn't capable of... It would have burned up in the atmosphere. It certainly couldn't have traveled through space."

Stan waved his hand. "Never mind that. You're right, but the technology. In the 1890s, Zeppelins were the big transportation craze."

"Until the Hindenburg," Martin offered.

"Among others. But the technology, Martin. Why were people seeing airships from Mars?"

Martin stared at him. "I have no idea. Mass hallucination?"

"Yes!" Stan said. "Or hype, as you call it. One town reports seeing an airship, and other towns want in on the story. It was an attention-grabber in a time when these towns all wanted to appear as though they were on the cutting edge of technologies like airships and...why Mars, Marty?"

Martin thought for a moment. Then it hit him. "Telescopes!" he said. Stan was nodding. "Telescopes had become household items and amateur astronomers could actually view Mars from their own backyards then. It was a hot topic in parlors and drawing rooms across the US."

Stan smiled. "That's it. Mars was big news. H. G. Welles was fueling the national imagination with books like *The Time Machine* and *War of the Worlds*, and people were fascinated by our little red neighbor. See, whatever the current edge of technology is, that's what people start seeing with their hype...and the hype eventually becomes our reality. After airships came airplanes, and within forty years, we had rockets. By the 1960s, we had astronauts. The atomic age, the space age. And what was on every Podunk newspaper's fifth page during that time?"

Martin thought for a moment and said, "Russians!"

Stan shook his head as he tried to take a sip of his drink. "No, no, Russians were usually first-page news, what with the Cuban missile crisis and all. What did people turn to, to escape that nuclear terror?"

"Movies?"

Stan moved his head to the side. "Yes, in some respect. I mean, Hollywood picked up these stories and ran with them, but what were the stories running in the papers then? Airships were 1890s, but the space age brought us..."

Martin got it. "Spaceships!"

"Spaceships, exactly. See, this 'hype' as you call it is often based on reality. Whatever the pinnacle of our technological abilities is, that's where imagination points us to the next step. These so-called mystery objects have been viewed throughout human history, but they are always described as something just one small step beyond our current technologies. Ezekiel saw wheels within wheels, Alexander the Great's armies saw flying shields, Zeppelin buffs of the 1890s saw Zeppelins, then when we reached space, people started seeing space-ships. And now that we are starting to study quantum physics and alternate universes, people are seeing beings from other dimensions. Whatever this 'hype' is we're chasing, it's always just one step ahead of us in our scientific understandings. First, the Stealth Bombers were seen as UFOs until the Air Force went public with them in the eighties. Now it's the Flying Triangles because they haven't told us about the TR-3B yet."

"The TR-3B? What sort of…"

"Never mind. The point is the correlation between 'hype' and 'reality,' Scoop. And that's what you're here to capture."

"Shouldn't you be Scoop?" Martin said in a sly attempt to escape his new moniker. "You're the reporter, after all."

"I know," Stan said, reaching down beside his seat. "That's why I got this cool hat." He produced a stylish reproduction of a '38 fedora. Sticking up from the headband was a white card that simply read "Press" in big, bold letters.

Marty smiled again. "Nice."

"It sure is, Scoop. And the ladies love it. Speaking of which…" He popped the hat onto his head when he saw the flight attendant returning. She smiled, and leaned in to tell him, "The flight crew told me to tell you welcome aboard, but none of them wishes to comment on any UFOs they may or may not have witnessed over the course of their careers."

"Are they drunk?" Stan inquired.

The attendant laughed a polite laugh. "No, sir. Our pilots never fly when they've been drinking."

"Have you seen any UFOs?"

"No, sir."

"Are you drunk?"

"No, sir."

"You wanna be? Want some of my G&T?"

"No, sir," the attendant replied, smiling a smile that said she might cut him off from the beverage cart at any moment. "Who did you say you write for?" she asked.

"The *Lone Nut*. It's not what you think. Our editor only has one ball."

"Really? Is it a periodical?"

"No, it's always there. It's just by itself."

"No, sir, I meant…" She could see her explanation would fall on deaf ears. She would have to watch this guy. He had had enough to drink, she thought. "Enjoy your flight," she said and returned to her duties.

"Thank you, Janet," Stan said as she walked back toward the crew cabin. "See that, Scoop? Ladies love the hat!"

In the seat by the window, Aaron had begun to snore.

A NOTE ON DRUG USE

Throughout this book, I tell of experiences I have had while using recreational drugs, some of which—such as psilocybin mushrooms and LSD—are very potent. Even the cannabis that is cultivated today has become much stronger than the variety we used in college, which was generally what was referred to as "dirt weed." I do not wish to suggest that the use of such drugs is a requirement for achieving a connection with the higher frequencies or for any type of enlightenment whatsoever. This just happened to be the path that I went down, simply because it was the culture that I had embraced at the time. And when I utilized these substances, I tried to do so as responsibly as I could. Even when taking "tour groups" out on LSD trips, I tried to do it in a controlled manner, similar to the LSD parties conducted by psychiatrists in the 1950s to 1960s before it was criminalized. These things are not to be trifled with. We used to shake our heads at people who would use them just for the escape, take them, and then go to parties and drink while under the influence of these powerful hallucinogens. It seemed a wasted opportunity and a reckless one at that. As I said, I have never had a "bad trip" on LSD or any other of these drugs, and I have never experienced a "flashback"—the idea that once you have taken a drug like LSD, you could suffer a relapse and experience hallucinations again at any given time out of the blue. I believe this to be nothing more than antidrug scare tactics promoted during the disastrous war on drugs, just another failed attempt by the oppressive forces to keep us removed from the collective, and to stifle our true spiritual power.

These days, drugs like cannabis sativa and psilocybin mushrooms are being given a second chance and have even been decriminalized in many places in the US and around the world. Many scientific studies have been produced that show that people suffering from PTSD or terminal illnesses tend to show an improved mental state upon ingesting psilocybin mushrooms or LSD. If you've understood the message of this book regarding death, then you can see evidence of such effects. Natural, organic drugs such as cannabis sativa, mushrooms, peyote, and ayahuasca are gifts (*hacks*, if you will) bestowed upon humanity to help us understand the larger world, a world within which we are still infants. We are housed in a sort of nursery in which we are meant to grow and learn, and these plants can offer us a window into the larger world within which we are meant to one day take a place. But I cannot stress the importance of responsible use enough. I will caution anyone that once they have learned what they need from these experiences, once there is no further feeling of enlightenment—no more flashing "*Aha!*" moments—they should stop taking these substances. Moderation in all things, as Henry Thoreau suggested.

As we used to joke in college, "We take drugs so you don't have to." Before embarking down the path of hallucinogens, try meditation, yoga, or breathing techniques like Pranayama. Experiment with sensory deprivation tanks or just lie flat on your back and listen to some chakra-aligning music on headphones, something in 432-hertz or 528-hertz range. As you lie there, extend your arms directly out in front of you and slowly move your fingers as though you are moving the energy around you. Then wrap your hands together and lower them onto your forehead, just at where you feel your third eye to be. See if any memories return, or any visions, or just enjoy the patterns on the backs of your eyelids. This sort of meditation can be done in your home, but it always works best if you are lying directly on the ground outside as the earth is a powerful conductor. The practice of "grounding" is very beneficial to your physical form as well as your spiritual. Use these methods in conjunction with one another and find what works best for you. And if you still wish to experiment with hallucinogens, start small. Try cannabis and see how it affects you. Always remember, it is important to be in a strong, positive place mentally and to be in good, trusted company physically. As I have said in the past, if I ever have a child and they come to me and say, "Dad, I'm either going to use the legal drug alcohol and get really drunk tonight, or I am going to break the law and smoke some weed," I would hope that they would break the law and smoke the weed. People who overindulge in alcohol can get sick, get into fights, car accidents, sleep with God knows who. But those who overindulge on weed might sit at home and binge on Ben & Jerry's and bad Netflix choices but generally be benevolent. Be responsible and remember to never put others at risk through your own behavior. *He who has ears, let him hear* (Matthew 11:15).

Now if you would indulge me a bit further, I would like to tell you of my experiences with a certain band that is famous for its music and also for the drug use within its surrounding culture: *the Grateful Dead*. It's not for everyone, but what is? This section is just to give some background as to how I came to believe that our minds are linked in some way. This was the soundtrack to my early years of experimental existence, and it helped to open my eyes to see how all things are connected. It started small—with a song in my head.

APPENDIX B

Grateful

I wanted to add this section for my own peace of mind. As you may have surmised from the book, I am a Deadhead—a fan of the band the Grateful Dead. As you also may have surmised from the book, I am a big believer in the collective consciousness ("God," if I may). These two facts about me overlap, and I would like to tell you how because I do believe it supports the collective consciousness theory.

Way back in the summer of 1990, three friends of mine and I piled into the Aerostar minivan that belonged to the parents of one of us, and we trucked it on up to Buffalo to see the Grateful Dead in concert. This was to be only the second concert of my young life and my first in a football stadium full of hippies. My first concert had been James Taylor at the Broome County Arena. At least, I think that's where it was. It felt more like a high school gymnasium. My memory is fuzzy.

Anyway, we headed up to Buffalo on one of the hottest days of that summer—I believe it was July 16. We were giddy. As we met the line of traffic two miles outside the stadium, things started moving slowly. So slow that Shakedown Street—the open market in which Deadheads trade and sell T-shirts, weed, tapes, hash, food and beverages, mushrooms, jewelry, pipes, LSD, and other accoutrements—opened right there on the highway. Deadheads walked from vehicle to vehicle, offering what they had. One fellow walked by mumbling the magic words our young ears were keen to hear: "Buds, doses..." Soon the fellow was in our van, the sliding doors closed, and my friends and I purchased five hits of LSD each. Our driver did not partake as, believe it or not, we were responsible to some extent. The rest of us dropped a tab, and I put my remaining four hits into the cellophane wrapper from my friend's cigarette pack and tucked them into my pocket. We bid our new friend farewell, and he ducked out with a friendly wave and a "See you at the show!"

Would we ever get to the show? Traffic was moving slower than a terrapin in tar, and the heat from the summer sun was starting to harm our ride. Soon, the minivan was belching blue smoke, and some Deadheads helped clear a path to the berm and assisted us in pushing the van out of traffic. Our driver assessed the situation and asked if the acid had kicked in yet. We told him it had not. He took our other more responsible friend with him to hike off the exit to a gas station and left the lesser-responsible (myself and the guy who had lost his key to the dorm in chapter 2) to watch the van. As we waited, I was touched by the generosity and kindness of Deadheads. Keep in mind, this was my first show. As traffic moved, new people arrived and came over to offer help. They opened the hood, examined the engine, told us we needed oil, more Deadheads came, gave us universal oil, more Deadheads came, brought us water...soon I had to pee. I walked down the embankment to a cluster of trees and relieved myself. As I stared at the bark of the tree in front of me, it moved. The tree was there with me. The acid was kicking in. I walked back up the embankment to where my friend was leaning against the back of the van. I started to say, "Hey, I think this acid is good!" but he just stared off into space and said, "Yep. Real good!" before I could utter a syllable. We both started laughing.

Soon our friends were back, and they also had universal motor oil. We topped off the van and prayed for a smooth ride off the exit to the garage. Somehow, we made it that far. The mechanic gave the engine the once-over and said that the van was done. It would travel no more. My friend, the responsible driver, asked if he could leave the van in the parking lot overnight as we had a show to get to. The mechanic was not happy about it, but he understood our situation, and permission was granted. We hitched a ride the rest of the way to the stadium in the back of a Deadhead's truck. My friend the driver was visibly disheartened. He said, "This sucks! Every time I go to see the Dead, something bad happens! Last time, I took a hit off a nitrous balloon and did a face-plant into the pavement. Broke my nose! Now this." Deadheads do not like to hear anything disparaging, especially on the way to a show, so people came around to cheer him up. One fellow cruised around us on Rollerblades, blowing bubbles, smiling, and saying, "The bubbles are free! The bubbles are free!" He came back around as we pulled into the parking lot. He had run out of bubble soap and was now just beaming at us, "The smiles are free! The smiles are free!"

We hopped out of the truck bed and thanked our kind host for the ride. "Don't mention it. Just have a great show!" We started to head into Shakedown Street Proper when we heard the sound *pssssssssshhhhhhhht!* and laughter. We followed. It was a dealer selling nitrous balloons out of the back of his van. We bought two big balloons. Now remember, we were young and stupid. Do not huff nitrous oxide. It is a tactical nuke on your brain cells. I am sure the writing of this book would be much more eloquent had it not been for that nitrous. At the time, however, it was just what the doctor (or dentist) had ordered. Our depressed driver took a big hit, turned to me with a big, stupid grin on his face, and said in the deep voice of frozen vocal cords, "I love you, man!" And we were off to never-never land.

Now, there is a thing I learned about at this show that Deadheads do that is called "Karma Pooling." The idea is to get your favorite song or any song you wanted to hear the Dead perform, stuck in as many heads as possible. If enough people walked into the show with your song on their minds, the Dead would play it. And *it worked*. I witnessed it on many occasions. A few people recognized us from the highway and said, "So glad you made it!" So were we! The Dead played Traffic's "Gimme Some Lovin'" late in the second set. That one was for us. To hear Bobby wailing, "So glad you made it!" was priceless. They opened the show with "Hell in a Bucket": "I may be going to hell in a bucket, babe, / but at least I'm enjoying the ride!" Check the set list, Rich Stadium, Buffalo, New York, July 16, 1990. It was a great show.

192

Bobby say, "We're gonna take a short break. We'll be right back."
And they walked right under us. There was a table of folded towels down there, and they were each grabbing one. I yelled, "Jerry!"
and Jerry Garcia looked up, grinned, and waved. That wasn't Karma
Pooling, that was just fuckin' *cool*.

I saw eleven shows before Jerry Garcia passed on August
9, 1995. That was such a sad day. I still feel blue to recall it. My
last show was that summer, in my beloved city of Pittsburgh. The
Grateful Dead had not been there for years, banned due to unruly
behavior by some bad-apple Deadheads. That summer of '95, they
were welcomed back with open arms. They played at Three Rivers
Stadium. My friend and I (the same guy who had guarded the van
with me at our first show) headed down from our sleepy college
town, taking the Thumb Express as neither of us had access to a
vehicle. We decided it would be better if we split up, as it is difficult
for two guys to get a ride together. I made it there in three rides. As
I was walking somewhere along 422, thumbing for my last ride, I
saw something green among the gray gravel. I picked it up. It was a
tiny ceramic turtle, one hand on its knee, the other raised palm-up,
eyes to the sky. It looked like it was missing a banjo. Later, when my
friends in Pittsburgh picked me up outside Number 1 Cochran, my
other hitchhiker friend was already sitting in the back seat. I handed
him the ceramic turtle and said, "They're gonna play Terrapin!" Sure
enough, second set, "Terrapin Station." They even opened the show
with "Hell in a Bucket," the same song they had opened my first
show with in '90. I had no idea at the time, however, that this was
going to be my last Jerry show.

That wasn't even the coolest part of that show. It was hot and
humid that day, and Deadheads were dropping like flies from heat
exhaustion. The opening act was a local band, Rusted Root, so everyone was inside to see the local boys open for the Grateful Dead, and
everyone was dancing their asses off before the Dead even came out.
And it was *hot*. And it was *humid*. Then the Dead came out, and
we danced our asses back on and off again. And Bobby said, "We're
gonna take a short break. We'll be right back." And it was *hot*. And it
was *humid*. And we all sat there in the stands, soaking in sweat, stew-

ing in our own juices, just a bunch of dirty, happy Deadheads, pray-ing, *praying*, for rain. We wanted a cool rain to break that oppressive humidity and give us life again so that we could keep dancing with-out anyone dying. And we waited in that humidity for the Dead to return. And we waited. And we waited. And it seemed like the Dead had skipped town to escape the humidity. But they wouldn't do that. Not to us. We were *family*, and we were all in this together. Slowly, one by one, the Dead reemerged. The crowd dragged itself to its feet, clapping rhythmically. The drummers Mickey and Bill got behind their kits and rumbled. The sky rumbled back. My friend leaned over to me, awe on his face, and said, "They're calling out the thunder!" I had my game face on, grinning from ear to ear, as I had managed to find acid on Shakedown Street. *Nothin' left to do but smile, smile, smile!* The rest of the band took up their positions…and just stood there. The crowd waited. Either the Dead had to play, or the rain had to come, but one way or another, one way or another, one way or another, that humidity had to *give*.

The Dead stepped to their mics, and in perfect *a cappella* har-mony, sang, "Rai-ai-ai-ai-aiain. I don't mind!" And the skies opened to a torrential downpour and the crowd. Went. Nuts. The Dead tore into the Beatles' "Rain" like children tearing into presents on Christmas morning, and the crowd cherished the gifts. The water kept falling, and the second set was mostly odes to the rain. When they blew up Three Rivers Stadium in 2001, I wasn't sad for the Steelers. I was sad for losing the landmark of my last Grateful Dead Show.

Thank you, Jerry.

One final note for safety: I have experimented with drugs. LSD is probably the hardest drug I have ever done, and I have done it on quite a few occasions. Let me just say that you don't need to use them to explore your mind/universe. If you choose them, do so with caution and be responsible. During the early nineties, we had a friend who met a guy who was a chemistry student at Lycoming College in Williamsport. This guy would sell us vials of liquid acid for fifty bucks. Each vial contained over one hundred doses of LSD, which we sold for three bucks a pop. We made a little money. And we made some incredible memories. It is hard to fight the temptation to tell you about some of my favorites here. This is not why I am writing this, however. During this time, friends would bring friends to my apartment, and we would take them on LSD adventures. We were cautious. Before dispensing the doses, we made sure everyone knew what they were in for: a twelve-hour ride into insanity and beyond. We covered some safety tips, told them that if anyone wandered off, keep an eye on them, use the buddy system. Don't let anyone get morose or lost in the dark. If they went off to sit by themselves, that's fine. Give them their space but watch for signs of panic. Do not return panic. Steer them back to the light with kindness, patience, and positive words. We had a code word to use if we rejoined "normal" society to let the others know at any time if we needed to get away and someone would walk with that person, or, ideally, we would all go. But you have to let people do their own thing on acid. Remember the Two Rules. When we dosed our tourists, as we called them, we immediately took them out of the town and up into the hills, into the trees and deer paths. There, they could safely lose their minds and come to grips with their new reality. Once they had peaked and had settled into their groove, we would slowly make our way back down the hill. By now, it was usually dark, so that helped us to blend in a bit. It was always fun to experience human society as tourists. I can see why so many entities do it. On the way down, we had a safe space to regroup, a hilltop above the campus band field that overlooked the town. *Look down there. See those lights? Real people down there. Are you ready to visit them?*

We called this hilltop the Top of the World. Sometimes we would decide we wanted nothing to do with the real people. We would just sit there on the Top of the World, looking at the stars, laughing. Then, all alone or in twos, we'd get tired, come down, and go home to sleep. One time, there were ten of us. One girl's beaded necklace broke, and she gathered up ten beads and gave one to each of us. The driver from my first Dead Show was with us, and he found a golf ball that became his buddy. As the tour group started to come down and people left, they would give their bead to someone who stayed with the group so that their presence among us would still be represented. By the break of dawn, there were three of us left, and we wandered down into town to go to the park. The joke that had us all laughing hysterically that morning was this: "Three students were stopped by police in the park today. They were found to be in possession of ten beads, a golf ball, and a groovy attitude." We chat on Facebook sometimes, those of us that were there, and that still makes us laugh (and now maybe cry a little bit too).

Take that with you: ten beads, a golf ball, and a groovy attitude.

> I've done a lot of drugs. I've had a lot of adventures on drugs, a lot of my music has been inspired by drugs. In fact, I think it's safe to say I've had some of the best times of my life on drugs. That doesn't mean YOU have to use them. (Eric Bogosian, "The Benefit" from *Sex, Drugs, Rock & Roll*)[1]

---

[1] You may have noticed by now, there is no big blue turtle.

ABOUT THE AUTHOR

Matthew Coleridge is an easily decipherable pseudonym for an expatriate who has been working and traveling abroad for the past thirteen years. Originally from Pennsylvania, USA, he holds an advanced degree in literary theory and has studied religion, philosophy, and several related subjects considered to be unusual or Fortean in nature, focusing mainly on extra- and ultraterrestrial phenomenon. He enjoys absurdist humor and currently resides in Asia.

9 781637 108185